COACHING YOUTH

LACROSSE

Endorsed by USL, Inc.

American Sport Education Program

Human Kinetics

Library of Congress Cataloging-in-Publication Data

American Sport Education Program.
   Coaching youth lacrosse / American Sport Education Program.
      p. cm.
   "Endorsed by USL, Inc."
   ISBN 0-88011-627-7
   1. Lacrosse for children.   2. Lacrosse--Coaching.   I. Title.
  GV989.17.A54 1997
  796.347'083--dc20   96-41428
                                                        CIP

ISBN: 0-88011-627-7

Artwork in appendices C and D is reprinted, by permission, from *The Lacrosse Foundation's Parent's Guide to the Sport of Lacrosse*, copyright © 1994, 1995, 1996 by The Lacrosse Foundation, Inc.

Acquisitions Editor: Jim Kestner; **Lacrosse Consultants:** Feffie Barnhill, College of William and Mary; Al Brown, Bates College; **Developmental Editor:** Jan Colarusso Seeley; **Assistant Editors:** Lynn M. Hooper, Coree Schutter, Jennifer Stallard; **Copyeditor:** Holly Gilly; **Proofreader:** Anne Meyer Byler; **Graphic Designer:** Judy Henderson; **Graphic Artist:** Francine Hamerski; **Cover Designer:** Stuart Cartwright; **Photographer (cover):** Bill Welch; **Illustrators:** John Hatton, line drawings; Jennifer Delmotte, Mac art; Tony Thamasangvarn, appendices C and D; **Printer:** United Graphics

Copies of this book are available at special discounts for bulk purchase for sales promotions, premiums, fund-raising, or educational use. Special editions or book excerpts can also be created to specifications. For details, contact the Special Sales Manager at Human Kinetics.

Printed in the United States of America   10 9 8 7 6 5 4 3 2 1

Human Kinetics
Web site: http://www.humankinetics.com/

United States: Human Kinetics
P.O. Box 5076
Champaign, IL 61825-5076
1-800-747-4457
e-mail: humank@hkusa.com

Canada: Human Kinetics, Box 24040
Windsor, ON N8Y 4Y9
1-800-465-7301 (in Canada only)
e-mail: humank@hkcanada.com

Europe: Human Kinetics, P.O. Box IW14
Leeds LS16 6TR, United Kingdom
(44) 1132 781708
e-mail: humank@hkeurope.com

Australia: Human Kinetics
57A Price Avenue
Lower Mitcham, South Australia 5062
(08) 277 1555
e-mail: humank@hkaustralia.com

New Zealand: Human Kinetics
P.O. Box 105-231, Auckland 1
(09) 523 3462
e-mail: humank@hknewz.com

Contents

A Message From USL, Inc.

Coaching Youth Lacrosse is a project initiated by the Lacrosse Foundation and now endorsed by USL, Inc. (United States Lacrosse, Inc.). This book is the first step in an ongoing effort by USL, Inc. to develop a comprehensive coaching education program for all levels of men's and women's lacrosse.

USL, Inc., the national governing body for the sport of lacrosse, would like to give a special thanks to authors Feffie Barnhill, Alfred Brown, Abigail Burbank, and Julia Mignatti for all their hard work in helping us create this valuable resource for youth lacrosse coaches. USL, Inc. would also like to thank the volunteers who helped review the book's original manuscript: Kim Basner, Drew Bowden, Pat Dillion, Mark Foster, Spook Hilgartner, David Huntley, Terry Kahn, Elaine Knobloch, Ruthie Lavelle, Larry Quinn, Sue Schooley, Craig Shirley, Steven B. Stenersen, Charlie Toomey, and Liz Wilson. Also deserving of special thanks is Bill Welch for providing the cover photography.

Most importantly we would like to thank you for your commitment to today's young athletes, and wish you many wonderful experiences while coaching youth lacrosse.

For more information about USL, Inc., please call, write, or e-mail us at

113 West University Parkway
Baltimore, MD 21210
(410) 235-6882
(410) 366-3675 (fax)
http://lacrosse.org

Welcome to Coaching!

Coaching young people is an exciting way to be involved in sport. But it isn't easy. Some coaches are overwhelmed by the responsibilities involved in helping athletes through their early sport experiences. And that's not surprising, because coaching youngsters requires more than bringing the sticks and balls to the field and letting them play. It involves preparing them physically and mentally to compete effectively, fairly, and safely in their sport, and providing them with a positive role model.

This book will help you meet the challenges *and* experience the many rewards of coaching young athletes. We call it *Coaching Youth Lacrosse* because it is intended for adults with little or no formal preparation in coaching lacrosse. In this book you'll learn how to apply general coaching principles and teach lacrosse rules, skills, and strategies successfully to kids. And while you may find that some of the information does not apply to your lacrosse program, we're confident this book will help you get a good jump on your coaching career.

The American Sport Education Program (ASEP) thanks USL, Inc. for contributing its lacrosse expertise to this book. Combined with ASEP's material on important coaching principles, this book covers all the bases.

This book also serves as a text for ASEP's Rookie Coaches Course. If you would like more information about this course or ASEP, please contact us at

ASEP
P.O. Box 5076
Champaign, IL 61825-5076
(800) 747-5698

Good Coaching!

Unit 1

Who, Me . . . a Coach?

If you are like most rookie coaches, you have probably been recruited from the ranks of concerned parents, sport enthusiasts, or community volunteers. And, like many rookie and veteran coaches, you probably have had little formal instruction on how to coach. But when the call went out for coaches to assist with the local youth lacrosse program, you answered because you like children and enjoy lacrosse, and because you want to be involved in a worthwhile community activity.

I Want to Help, but . . .

Your initial coaching assignment may be difficult. Like many volunteers, you may not know everything there is to know about lacrosse, nor about how to work with children between the ages of 6 and 14. Relax, because *Coaching Youth Lacrosse* will help you learn the basics for coaching lacrosse effectively. In the coming pages you will find the answers to such common questions as these:

- What tools do I need to be a good coach?
- How can I best communicate with my players?
- How do I go about teaching sport skills?
- What can I do to promote safety?
- What should I do when someone is injured?
- What are the basic rules, skills, and strategies of lacrosse?
- What practice drills will improve my players' lacrosse skills?

Before answering these questions, let's take a look at what's involved in being a coach.

Am I a Parent or a Coach?

Many coaches are parents, but the two roles should not be confused. Unlike your role as a parent, as a coach you are responsible not only to yourself and your child, but also to the organization, all the players on the team (including your child), and their parents. Because of this additional responsibility, your behavior on the playing field will be different from your behavior at home, and your son or daughter may not understand why.

For example, imagine the confusion of a young boy who is the center of his parents' attention at home but is barely noticed by his parent/coach in the sport setting. Or consider the mixed signals received by a young girl whose lacrosse skill is constantly evaluated by a parent/coach who otherwise rarely comments on her daughter's activities. You need to explain to your son or daughter your new responsibilities and how they will affect your relationship when coaching.

Take the following steps to avoid such problems in coaching your child:

- Ask your child if he or she wants you to coach the team.
- Explain why you wish to be involved with the team.
- Discuss with your child how your interactions will change when you take on the role of coach at practices or games.
- Limit your coaching behavior to when you are in the coaching role.
- Avoid parenting during practice or game situations, to keep your role clear in your child's mind.
- Reaffirm your love for your child, irrespective of his or her performance on the lacrosse field.

What Are My Responsibilities as a Coach?

A coach assumes the responsibility of doing everything possible to ensure that the youngsters on his or her team will have an enjoyable and safe sporting experience while they learn sport skills. If you're ever in doubt about your approach, remind yourself that "fun and fundamentals" are most important.

Provide an Enjoyable Experience

Lacrosse should be fun. Even if nothing else is accomplished, make certain your players have fun. Take the fun out of sport and you'll take the kids out of sport.

Children enter sport for a number of reasons (e.g., to meet and play with other children, to develop physically, and to learn skills), but their major objective is to have fun. Help them satisfy this goal by injecting humor and variety into your practices. Also, make games nonthreatening, festive experiences for your players. Such an approach will increase your players' desire to participate in the future, which should be the biggest goal of youth sport. Unit 2 will help you learn how to satisfy your players' yearning for fun and keep winning in perspective. And unit 3 will describe how you can effectively communicate this perspective to them.

Provide a Safe Experience

You are responsible for planning and teaching activities in such a way that the progression between activities minimizes risks (see units 4 and 5). Further, you must ensure that the field on which your team practices and plays, and the equipment team members use, are free of hazards. Finally, you need to protect yourself from any legal liability issues that might arise from your involvement as a coach. Unit 5 will help you take the appropriate precautions.

Provide Opportunities for Children With Disabilities

There's a possibility that a child with a disability of some kind will register for your team. Don't panic! Your youth sport administrator or a number of organizations (see appendix E) can provide you with information to help you best meet this child's needs.

As a coach, you need to know about the Americans with Disabilities Act (ADA). Passed in 1990, the ADA gives individuals the same legal protection against discrimination on the basis of disabilities as is provided against discrimination on the basis of race, gender, and class. The law does recognize that there are times when including an individual who is disabled might risk the safety of that individual and other players, but the exact way that courts are treating the ADA is still being decided. In general, the law requires that "reasonable accommodations" be made to include children with disabilities into organized sport programs. If a parent or child approaches you on the subject, and you aren't sure what to do, talk to the director in charge of your lacrosse program. If you make any decision on your own pertaining to the ADA, you may be vulnerable to a lawsuit.

Keep in mind that these children want to participate alongside their able-bodied peers. Give them the same support and encouragement that you give other athletes, and model their inclusion and acceptance for all your athletes.

Teach Basic Lacrosse Skills

In becoming a coach, you take on the role of educator. You must teach your players the fundamental skills and strategies necessary for success in lacrosse. That means that you need to "go to school."

If you don't know the basics of lacrosse now, you can learn them by reading the second half of this book, units 6-12. But even if you know lacrosse as a player, do you know how to teach it? This book will help you get started.

You'll also find it easier to provide good educational experiences for your players if you plan your practices. Unit 4 of this book provides some guidelines for planning effective practices.

Getting Help

Veteran coaches in your league are an especially good source of help for you. These coaches have all experienced the same emotions and concerns you are facing, and their advice and feedback can be invaluable as you work through your first season.

You can also learn a lot by watching local high school and college lacrosse coaches in practices and games. You might even ask a few of the coaches you respect most to lend you a hand with a couple of your practices. You can get

additional help by attending lacrosse clinics, reading lacrosse publications, and studying instructional videos. In addition to the American Sport Education Program (ASEP), the following national organizations will assist you in obtaining more lacrosse coaching information:

United States Lacrosse Coaches
  Association
c/o Tony Seaman
Johns Hopkins University
Charles Street and 34th Street
Baltimore, MD 21218
(410) 516-7479

USL, Inc.
113 West University Parkway
Baltimore, MD 21210
(410) 235-6882

National Junior Lacrosse
  Association
113 West University Parkway
Baltimore, MD 21210
(410) 235-6882

United States Women's Lacrosse
  Association
Home Office
P.O. Box 2178
Amherst, MA 01004
(413) 253-0328

Intercollegiate Women's Lacrosse
  Coaches Association
Andrea Golden
Harvard University
60 Kennedy Street
Cambridge, MA 02138
(617) 492-2762

Coaching lacrosse is a rewarding experience. And, just as you want your players to learn and practice to be the best they can be, you need to learn all you can about coaching in order to be the best lacrosse coach you can be.

What Tools Do I Need as a Coach?

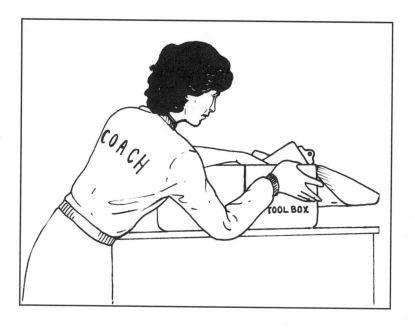

Have you purchased the traditional coaching tools—things like whistles, coaching clothes, sport shoes, and a clipboard? They'll help you coach, but to be a successful coach you'll need five other tools that cannot be bought. These tools are available only through self-examination and hard work; they're easy to remember using the acronym COACH:

C—Comprehension

O—Outlook

A—Affection

C—Character

H—Humor

Comprehension

Comprehension of the rules, skills, and tactics of lacrosse is required. To help you learn about the game, the second half of this book describes rules, skills, and tactics of lacrosse and suggests how to plan for the season and for individual practices. In the lacrosse-specific section of this book, you'll also find a variety of drills to use in developing young players' skills. And, perhaps most important, you'll learn how to apply your knowledge of the game to teach your lacrosse team.

To improve your comprehension of lacrosse, take the following steps:

- Read the lacrosse-specific section of this book.
- Read other lacrosse coaching books, including those available from USL, Inc. Call (410) 235-6882.
- Contact any of the organizations listed on page 6.
- Attend lacrosse coaches' clinics.
- Talk with other, more experienced, lacrosse coaches.
- Observe local college, high school, and youth lacrosse games.
- Watch lacrosse games on television.

In addition to having lacrosse knowledge, you must implement proper training and safety methods so your players can participate with little risk of injury. Even then, sport injuries will occur. And more often than not, you'll be the first person responding to your players' injuries, so be sure you understand the basic emergency care procedures described in unit 5. Also, read in that unit how to handle more serious sport injury situations.

Outlook

Outlook refers to your perspective and goals—what you are seeking as a coach. The most common coaching objectives are (a) to have fun, (b) to help players develop their physical, mental, and social skills, and (c) to win. Thus your outlook involves the priorities you set, your planning, and your vision for the future.

To work successfully with children in a sport setting, you must have your priorities in order. In just what order do you rank the importance of fun, development, and winning?

Answer the following questions to examine your objectives:

Of which situation would you be most proud?

 a. Knowing that each participant enjoyed playing lacrosse.
 b. Seeing that all players improved their lacrosse skills.
 c. Winning the league championship.

Which statement best reflects your thoughts about sport?

 a. If it isn't fun, don't do it.
 b. Everyone should learn something every day.
 c. Sport isn't fun if you don't win.

How would you like your players to remember you?

 a. As a coach who was fun to play for.
 b. As a coach who provided a good base of fundamental skills.
 c. As a coach who had a winning record.

Which would you most like to hear a parent of a child on your team say?

 a. Billy really had a good time playing lacrosse this year.
 b. Susie learned some important lessons playing lacrosse this year.
 c. Jose played on the first-place lacrosse team this year.

Which of the following would be the most rewarding moment of your season?

 a. Having your team want to continue playing, even after practice is over.
 b. Seeing one of your players finally master the skill of passing.
 c. Winning the league championship.

Look over your answers. If you most often selected "a" responses, then having fun is most important to you. A majority of "b" answers suggests that skill development is what attracts you to coaching. And if "c" was your most frequent response, winning is tops on your list of coaching priorities.

Most coaches say fun and development are more important, but when actually coaching, some coaches emphasize—indeed, overemphasize—winning. You, too, will face situations that challenge you to keep winning in its proper perspective. During such moments, you'll have to choose between emphasizing your players' development or winning. If your priorities are in order, your players' well-being will take precedence over your team's win-loss record every time.

Take the following actions to better define your outlook:

1. Determine your priorities for the season.
2. Prepare for situations that challenge your priorities.
3. Set goals for yourself and your players that are consistent with those priorities.

4. Plan how you and your players can best attain those goals.

5. Review your goals frequently to be sure that you are staying on track.

It is particularly important for coaches to permit all young athletes to participate. Each youngster—male or female, small or tall, gifted or disabled—should have an opportunity to develop skills and have fun.

Remember that the challenge and joy of sport is experienced through striving to win, not through winning itself. Players who aren't allowed off the bench are denied the opportunity to strive to win. And herein lies the irony: Coaches who allow all of their players to participate and develop skills will—in the end—come out on top.

ASEP has a motto that will help you keep your outlook in the best interest of the kids on your team. It summarizes in four words all you need to remember when establishing your coaching priorities:

Athletes First,

Winning Second

This motto recognizes that striving to win is an important, even vital, part of sport. But it emphatically states that no efforts in striving to win should be made at the expense of the athletes' well-being, development, and enjoyment.

Affection

Affection is another vital tool you will want to have in your coaching kit: a genuine concern for the young people you coach. It involves having a love for children, a desire to share with them your love and knowledge of lacrosse, and the patience and understanding that allow each individual playing for you to grow from his or her involvement in lacrosse.

Successful coaches have a real concern for the health and welfare of their players. They care that each child on the team has an enjoyable and successful experience. They recognize that there are similarities between young people's sport experiences and other activities in their lives, and they encourage their players to strive to learn from all their experiences, to become well-rounded individuals. These coaches have a strong desire to work with children and be involved in their growth. And they have the patience to work with those who are slower to learn or less capable of performing. If you have such qualities or are willing to work hard to develop them, then you have the affection necessary to coach young athletes.

There are many ways to demonstrate your affection and patience, including these:

- Make an effort to get to know each player on your team.
- Treat each player as an individual.

- Empathize with players trying to learn new and difficult lacrosse skills.
- Treat players as you would like to be treated under similar circumstances.
- Be in control of your emotions.
- Show your enthusiasm for being involved with your team.
- Keep an upbeat and positive tone in all of your communications.

Some children appreciate a pat on the back or shoulder as a sign of your approval or affection. But be aware that not all players feel comfortable with being touched. When this is the case, you need to respect their wishes.

Character

Character is a word that adults use frequently in conversations about sport experiences and young people. If you haven't already, you may one day be asked to explain whether you think sport builds good character. What will you say?

The fact that you have decided to coach young lacrosse players probably means that you think participation in sport is important. But whether or not that participation develops character in your players depends as much on you as it does on the sport itself. How can you build character in your players?

Youngsters learn by listening to what adults say. But they learn even more by watching the behavior of certain important individuals. As a coach, you are likely to be a significant figure in the lives of your players. Will you be a good role model?

Having good character means modeling appropriate behaviors for sport and life. That means more than just saying the right things. What you say and what you do must match. There is no place in coaching for the "Do as I say, not as I do" philosophy. Challenge, support, encourage, and reward every child, and your players will be more likely to accept, even celebrate, their differences. Be in control before, during, and after all games and practices. And don't be afraid to admit that you were wrong. No one is perfect!

Many of us have been coached by someone who believes that criticizing players is a good way to build character. In reality, this approach damages children's self-esteem and teaches them that their value as a person is based on how they perform in sport. Unit 3 will help you communicate with your players in a way that builds positive self-esteem and develops your athletes' skills.

Finally, take stock of your own attitudes about ethnic, gender, and other stereotypes. You are an individual coach, and it would be wrong for others to form beliefs about you based on their personal attitudes about coaches in general. Similarly, you need to avoid making comments that support stereotypes of others. Let your words and actions show your players that every individual matters, and you will be teaching them a valuable lesson about respecting and supporting individuals' differences.

Consider the following steps to being a good role model:

- Take stock of your strengths and weaknesses.
- Build on your strengths.
- Set goals for yourself to improve upon those areas you would not like to see mimicked.

- If you slip up, apologize to your team and to yourself. You'll do better next time.

Humor

Humor is an often-overlooked coaching tool. For our use it means having the ability to laugh at yourself and with your players during practices and games. Nothing helps balance the tone of a serious, skill-learning session like a chuckle or two. And a sense of humor puts in perspective the many mistakes your young players will make. So don't get upset over each miscue or respond negatively to erring players. Allow your players and yourself to enjoy the ups, and don't dwell on the downs.

Here are some tips for injecting humor into your practices:

- Make practices fun by including a variety of activities.
- Keep all players involved in drills and scrimmages.
- Consider laughter by your players a sign of enjoyment, not waning discipline.
- Smile!

Where Do You Stand?

To take stock of your "coaching tool kit," rank yourself on the three questions for each of the five coaching tools. Simply circle the number that best describes your current status on each item.

Not at all		Somewhat		Very much so
1	2	3	4	5

Comprehension _____

1. Could you explain the rules of lacrosse to other parents without studying for a long time?   1 2 3 4 5
2. Do you know how to organize and conduct safe lacrosse practices?   1 2 3 4 5
3. Do you know how to provide first aid for most common, minor sport injuries?   1 2 3 4 5

Comprehension Score: _____

Outlook

4. Do you place the interests of all children ahead of winning when you coach?   1 2 3 4 5
5. Do you plan for every meeting, practice, and game?   1 2 3 4 5
6. Do you have a vision of what you want your players to be able to do by the end of the season?   1 2 3 4 5

Outlook Score: _____

Affection

7. Do you enjoy working with children?   1 2 3 4 5
8. Are you patient with youngsters learning new skills?   1 2 3 4 5
9. Are you able to show your players that you care?   1 2 3 4 5

Affection Score: _____

Character

10. Are your words and behaviors consistent with each other?   1 2 3 4 5
11. Are you a good model for your players?   1 2 3 4 5
12. Do you keep negative emotions under control before, during, and after contests?   1 2 3 4 5

Character Score: _____

Humor

13. Do you usually smile at your players?   1 2 3 4 5
14. Are your practices fun?   1 2 3 4 5
15. Are you able to laugh at your mistakes?   1 2 3 4 5

Humor Score: _____

If you scored 9 or less on any of the coaching tools, be sure to reread those sections carefully. And even if you scored 15 on each tool, don't be complacent. Keep learning! Then you'll be well-equipped with the tools you need to coach young athletes.

Unit 3

How Should I Communicate With My Players?

Now you know the tools needed to COACH: Comprehension, Outlook, Affection, Character, and Humor. These are essentials for effective coaching; without them, you'd have a difficult time getting started. But none of those tools will work if you don't know how to use them with your athletes—and this requires skillful communication. This unit examines what communication is and how you can become a more effective communicator-coach.

What's Involved in Communication?

Coaches often mistakenly believe that communication involves only instructing players to do something, but verbal commands are a very small part of the communication process. More than half of what is communicated is nonverbal. So remember when you are coaching: Actions speak louder than words.

Communication in its simplest form involves two people: a sender and a receiver. The sender transmits the message verbally, through facial expression, and possibly through body language. Once the message is sent, the receiver must try to determine the meaning of the message. A receiver who fails to attend or listen will miss parts, if not all, of the message.

How Can I Send More Effective Messages?

Young athletes often have little understanding of the rules and skills of lacrosse and probably even less confidence in playing it. So they need accurate, understandable, and supportive messages to help them along. That's why your verbal and nonverbal messages are so important.

Verbal Messages

"Sticks and stones may break my bones, but words will never hurt me" isn't true. Spoken words can have a strong and long-lasting effect. And coaches' words are particularly influential because youngsters place great importance on what coaches say. Perhaps you, like many former youth sport participants, have a difficult time remembering much of anything you were told by your elementary school teachers but can still recall several specific things your coaches at that level said to you. Such is the lasting effect of a coach's comments to a player.

Whether you are correcting misbehavior, teaching a player how to pass the ball, or praising a player for good effort, there are a number of things you should consider when sending a message verbally. They include the following:

- *Be positive and honest.*

- *State it clearly and simply.*
- *Say it loud enough, and say it again.*
- *Be consistent.*

Be Positive and Honest

Nothing turns people off like hearing someone nag all the time, and young athletes react similarly to a coach who gripes constantly. Kids particularly need encouragement because many of them doubt their ability to play lacrosse. So look for and tell your players what they did well.

But don't cover up poor or incorrect play with rosy words of praise. Kids know all too well when they've erred, and no cheerfully expressed cliché can undo their mistakes. If you fail to acknowledge players' errors, your athletes will think you are a phony.

COMPLIMENT SANDWICH

A good way to handle situations in which you have identified and must correct improper technique is to serve your players a "compliment sandwich":

1. Point out what the athlete did correctly.
2. Let the player know what was incorrect in the performance and instruct him or her how to correct it.
3. Encourage the player by reemphasizing what he or she did well.

State It Clearly and Simply

Positive and honest messages are good, but only if expressed directly in words your players understand. "Beating around the bush" is ineffective and inefficient. And if you do ramble, your players will miss the point of your message and probably lose interest. Here are some tips for saying things clearly:

- Organize your thoughts before speaking to your athletes.
- Explain things thoroughly, but don't bore them with long-winded monologues.
- Use language your players can understand. However, avoid trying to be hip by using their age group's slang vocabulary.

Say It Loud Enough, and Say It Again

A lacrosse field with kids spread out can make communication difficult. So talk to your team in a voice that all members can hear and interpret. A crisp, vigorous voice commands attention and respect; garbled and weak speech is tuned out. It's OK, in fact, appropriate, to soften your voice when speaking to a player individually about a personal problem. But most of the time your messages will be for all your players to hear, so make sure they can! An enthusiastic voice also motivates players and tells them you enjoy being their coach. A word of caution, however: Don't dominate the setting with a booming voice that distracts attention from players' performances.

Sometimes what you say, even if stated loud and clear, won't sink in the first time. This may be particularly true with young athletes hearing words

they don't understand. To avoid boring repetition and yet still get your message across, say the same thing in a slightly different way. For instance, you might first tell your players "Force your opponent to her weak side." Soon afterward, remind them to "Be in good defensive position so you can deny the ball strong side, and if your opponent catches the ball she will be forced to use her non-dominant hand." The second form of the message may get through to players who missed it the first time around.

Be Consistent

People often say things in ways that imply a different message. For example, a touch of sarcasm added to the words "way to go" sends an entirely different message than the words themselves suggest. It is essential that you avoid sending such mixed messages. Keep the tone of your voice consistent with the words you use. And don't say something one day and contradict it the next; players will get confused. If you still aren't certain whether your players understand, ask them to repeat the message back to you. As the old saying goes "If they can't say it, they can't play it."

Nonverbal Messages

Just as you should be consistent in the tone of voice and words you use, you should also keep your verbal and nonverbal messages consistent. An extreme example of failing to do this would be shaking your head, indicating disapproval, while at the same time telling a player "Nice try." Which is the player to believe, your gesture or your words?

Messages can be sent nonverbally in a number of ways. Facial expressions and body language are just two of the more obvious forms of nonverbal signals that can help you when you coach.

Facial Expressions

The look on a person's face is the quickest clue to what he or she thinks or feels. Your players know this, so they will study your face, looking for any sign that will tell them more than the words you say. Don't try to fool them by putting on a happy or blank "mask." They'll see through it, and you'll lose credibility.

Serious, stone-faced expressions are no help to kids who need cues as to how they are performing. They will just assume you're unhappy or disinterested. Don't be afraid to smile. A smile from a coach can give a great boost to an unsure young athlete. Plus, a smile lets your players know that you are happy coaching them. But don't overdo it, or your players won't be able to tell when you are genuinely pleased by something they've done or when you are just putting on a smiling face.

Body Language

What would your players think you were feeling if you came to practice slouched over, with head down and shoulders slumped? Tired? Bored? Unhappy? What would they think you were feeling if you watched them during a contest with your hands on your hips, your jaws clenched, and your face reddened? Upset with them? Disgusted at an official? Mad at a fan? Probably some or all of these things would enter your players' minds. And none of these impressions is the kind you want your players to have of you. That's why you should carry yourself in a pleasant, confident, and vigorous manner. Such a posture not only projects happiness with your coaching role but also provides a good example for your young players who may model your behavior.

Physical contact can also be a very important use of body language. A handshake, a pat on the back, an arm around the shoulder, or even a big hug are effective ways of showing approval, concern, affection, and joy to your players. Youngsters are especially in need of this type of nonverbal message. Keep within the obvious moral and legal limits, but don't be reluctant to touch your players and send a message that can only truly be expressed in that way.

How Can I Improve My Receiving Skills?

Now, let's examine the other half of the communication process—receiving messages. Too often people are very good senders but very poor receivers of messages. As a coach of young athletes, it is essential that you are able to fulfill both roles effectively.

The requirements for receiving messages are quite simple, but receiving skills are perhaps less satisfying and therefore underdeveloped compared to sending skills. People seem to naturally enjoy hearing themselves talk more than others. But if you are willing to read about the keys to receiving messages and to make a strong effort to use them with your players, you'll be surprised by what you've been missing.

Attention!

First, you must pay attention; you must want to hear what others have to communicate to you. That's not always easy when you're busy coaching and have many things competing for your attention. But in one-to-one or team meetings with players, you must really focus on what they are telling you, both verbally and nonverbally. You'll be amazed at the little signals you pick up. Not only will such focused attention help you catch every word your players say, but you'll also notice your players' moods and physical states, and you'll get an idea of your players' feelings toward you and other players on the team.

Listen CARE-FULLY

How we receive messages from others, perhaps more than anything else we do, demonstrates how much we care for the sender and what that person has to tell us. If you care little for your players or have little regard for what they have to say, it will show in how you attend and listen to them. Check yourself. Do you find your mind wandering to what you are going to do after practice while one of your players is talking to you? Do you frequently have to ask your players, "What did you say?" If so, you need to work on your receiving mechanics of attending and listening. But perhaps the most critical question you should ask yourself, if you find that you're missing the messages your players send, is this: Do I care?

How Do I Put It All Together?

So far we've discussed separately the sending and receiving of messages. But we all know that senders and receivers switch roles several times during an interaction. One person initiates a communication by sending a message to another person, who then receives the message. The receiver then switches roles and becomes the sender by responding to the person who sent the initial message. These verbal and nonverbal responses are called feedback.

Your players will be looking to you for feedback all the time. They will want to know how you think they are performing, what you think of their ideas, and whether their efforts please you. Obviously, you can respond in many different ways. How you respond will strongly affect your players. So let's take a look at a few general types of feedback and examine their possible effects.

Providing Instructions

With young players, much of your feedback will involve answering questions about how to play lacrosse. Your instructive responses to these questions should include both verbal and nonverbal feedback. Here are some suggestions for giving instructional feedback:

- Keep verbal instructions simple and concise.
- Use demonstrations to provide nonverbal instructional feedback (see unit 4).
- "Walk" players through the skill, or use a slow-motion demonstration if they are having trouble learning.

Correcting Errors

When your players perform incorrectly, you need to provide informative feedback to correct the error—and the sooner the better. When you do correct errors, keep in mind these two principles: Use negative criticism sparingly, and keep calm.

Use Negative Criticism Sparingly

Although you may need to punish players for horseplay or dangerous activities by scolding or removing them from activity temporarily, avoid reprimanding players for performance errors. Admonishing players for honest mistakes makes them afraid to even try. Nothing ruins a youngster's enjoyment of a sport more than a coach who harps on every mistake. So instead, correct your players by using the positive approach. Your players will enjoy playing more, and you'll enjoy coaching more.

Keep Calm

Don't fly off the handle when your players make mistakes. Remember, you're coaching young and inexperienced players, not pros. You'll therefore see more incorrect than correct technique, and you'll probably have more discipline problems than you expect. But throwing a tantrum over each error or misbehavior will only inhibit your players or suggest to them the wrong kind of behavior to model. So let your players know that mistakes aren't the end of the world; stay cool!

Giving Positive Feedback

Praising players when they have performed or behaved well is an effective way of getting them to repeat (or try to repeat) that behavior in the future. And positive feedback for effort is an especially effective way to motivate youngsters to work on difficult skills. So rather than shouting and providing negative feedback to a player who has made a mistake, try offering players a compliment sandwich, described on page 18.

Sometimes just the way you word feedback can make it more positive than negative. For example, instead of saying, "Don't drop the ball," you might

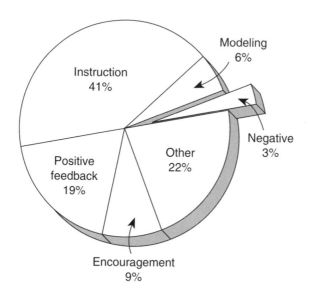

Coaches, be positive!

Only a very small percentage of ASEP-trained coaches' behaviors are negative.

Modeling 6%

Instruction 41%

Negative 3%

Positive feedback 19%

Other 22%

Encouragement 9%

say, "Cradle the ball with both hands." Then your players will be focusing on what to do instead of what not to do.

You can give positive feedback verbally and nonverbally. Telling a player, especially in front of teammates, that he or she has performed well is a great way to boost the youngster's confidence. A pat on the back or a handshake can be a very tangible way of communicating your recognition of a player's performance.

Who Else Do I Need to Communicate With?

Coaching involves not only sending and receiving messages and providing proper feedback to players, but also interacting with parents, fans, game officials, and opposing coaches. If you don't communicate effectively with these groups of people, your coaching career will be unpleasant and short-lived. So try the following suggestions for communicating with these groups.

Parents

A player's parents need to be assured that their son or daughter is under the direction of a coach who is both knowledgeable about lacrosse and concerned about the youngster's well-being. You can put their worries to rest by holding a preseason parent orientation meeting in which you describe your background and your approach to coaching.

If parents contact you with a concern during the season, listen to them closely and try to offer positive responses. If you need to communicate with parents, catch them after a practice, give them a phone call, or send a note through the mail. Messages sent to parents through children are too often lost, misinterpreted, or forgotten.

Fans

The stands probably won't be overflowing at your contests, but that only means that you'll more easily hear the few fans who criticize your coaching. When you hear something negative said about the job you're doing, don't respond. Keep calm, consider whether the message has any value, and if not, forget it. Acknowledging critical, unwarranted comments from a fan during a contest will only encourage others to voice their opinions. So put away your "rabbit ears" and communicate to fans, through your actions, that you are a confident, competent coach.

Even if you are ready to withstand the negative comments of fans, your players may not be. Prepare your players for fans' criticisms. Tell them it is you, not the spectators, to whom they should listen. If you notice that one of your players is rattled by a fan's comment, reassure the player that your evaluation is more objective and favorable—and the one that counts.

Game Officials

How you communicate with officials will have a great influence on the way your players behave toward them. Therefore, you need to set an example. Greet officials with a handshake, an introduction, and perhaps some casual conversation about the upcoming contest. Indicate your respect for them before, during, and after the game. Don't make nasty remarks, shout, or use disrespectful body gestures. Your players will see you do it, and they'll get the idea that such behavior is appropriate. Plus, if the official hears or sees you, the communication between the two of you will break down.

Opposing Coaches

Make an effort to visit with the coach of the opposing team before the game. Perhaps the two of you can work out a special arrangement for the game, such as free subsitution of players. During the game, don't get into a personal feud with the opposing coach. Remember, it's the kids, not the coaches, who are competing. And by getting along well with the opposing coach, you'll show your players that competition involves cooperation.

✔ *Summary Checklist*

Now, check your coach-communication skills by answering "Yes" or "No" to the following questions.

                                                                    Yes   No

1. Are your verbal messages to your players positive and honest?

2. Do you speak loudly, clearly, and in a language your athletes understand?

3. Do you remember to repeat instructions to your players, in case they didn't hear you the first time?

4. Are the tone of your voice and your nonverbal messages consistent with the words you use?

5. Do your facial expressions and body language express interest in and happiness with your coaching role?

6. Are you attentive to your players and able to pick up even their small verbal and nonverbal cues?

7. Do you really care about what your athletes say to you?

8. Do you instruct rather than criticize when your players make errors?

9. Are you usually positive when responding to things your athletes say and do?

10. Do you try to communicate in a cooperative and respectful manner with players' parents, fans, game officials, and opposing coaches?

If you answered "No" to any of the above questions, you may want to refer back to the section of the chapter where the topic was discussed. Now is the time to address communication problems, not when you're on the field with your players.

Unit 4

How Do I Get My Team Ready to Play?

To coach lacrosse, you must understand the basic rules, skills, and strategies. The second part of this book provides the basic information you'll need to comprehend the sport.

But all the lacrosse knowledge in the world will do you little good unless you present it effectively to your players. That's why this unit is so important. Here you will learn the steps to take when teaching sport skills, as well as practical guidelines for planning your season and individual practices.

How Do I Teach Lacrosse Skills?

Many people believe that the only qualification needed to coach is to have played the sport. It's helpful to have played, but there is much more to coaching successfully. Even if you haven't played or even watched lacrosse, you can still learn to coach successfully with this IDEA:

I—Introduce the skill.

D—Demonstrate the skill.

E—Explain the skill.

A—Attend to players practicing the skill.

Introduce the Skill

Players, especially young and inexperienced ones, need to know what skill they are learning and why they are learning it. You should therefore take these three steps every time you introduce a skill to your players:

1. Get your players' attention.
2. Name the skill.
3. Explain the importance of the skill.

Get Your Players' Attention

Because youngsters are easily distracted, use some method to get their attention. Some coaches use interesting news items or stories. Others use jokes. And others simply project enthusiasm that gets their players to listen. Whatever method you use, speak slightly above the normal volume and look your players in the eyes when you speak.

Also, position players so they can see and hear you. Arrange the players in two or three evenly spaced rows, facing you and not the sun or some source of distraction. Then ask if everyone can see and hear you before you begin.

Name the Skill

Although you might mention other common names for the skill, decide which one you'll use and stick with it. This will help avoid confusion and enhance communication among your players. For example, choose either "clear" or "break" as the term the goalie says after a save, and use it consistently.

Explain the Importance of the Skill

Although the importance of a skill may be apparent to you, your players may be less able to see how the skill will help them become better lacrosse players. Offer them a reason for learning the skill and describe how the skill relates to more advanced skills.

> "The most difficult aspect of coaching is this: Coaches must learn to let athletes learn. Sport skills should be taught so they have meaning to the child, not just meaning to the coach."
>
> Rainer Martens, ASEP Founder

Demonstrate the Skill

The demonstration step is the most important part of teaching a lacrosse skill to young players who may have never done anything closely resembling it. They need a picture, not just words. They need to see how the skill is performed.

If you are unable to perform the skill correctly, have an assistant coach, one of your players, or someone skilled in lacrosse perform the demonstration. These tips will help make your demonstrations more effective:

- Use correct form.
- Demonstrate the skill several times.
- Slow down the action, if possible, during one or two performances so players can see every movement involved in the skill.
- Perform the skill at different angles so your players can get a full perspective of it.
- Demonstrate the skill with both the right and left hands.

Explain the Skill

Players learn more effectively when they're given a brief explanation of the skill along with the demonstration. Use simple terms to describe the skill and, if possible, relate it to previously learned skills. Ask your players whether they understand your description. A good technique is to ask the team to repeat your explanation. Ask questions like "What are you going to do first?" "Then what?" Watch for looks of confusion or uncertainty and repeat your explanation and demonstration of those points. If possible, use different words so that your players get a chance to try to understand from a different perspective.

Complex skills often are better understood when they are explained in more manageable parts. For instance, if you want to teach your players how to change direction when they cradle the ball, you might take the following steps:

1. Show them a correct performance of the entire skill and explain its function in lacrosse.

2. Break down the skill and point out its component parts to your players.

3. Have players perform each of the component skills you have already taught them, such as cradling while dodging or switching hands while keeping their heads up.

4. After players have demonstrated their ability to perform the separate parts of the skill in sequence, reexplain the entire skill.

5. Have players practice the skill.

One caution: Young players have short attention spans, and a long demonstration or explanation of the skill will bore them. So spend no more than a few minutes combined on the introduction, demonstration, and explanation phases. Then get the players active in attempts to perform the skill. The total

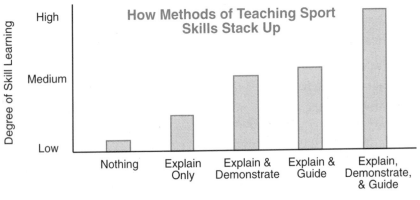

Coaches' Teaching Methods

IDEA should be completed in 10 minutes or less, followed by individual and group practice activities.

Attend to Players Practicing the Skill

If the skill you selected was within your players' capabilities, and you have done an effective job of introducing, demonstrating, and explaining it, your players should be ready to attempt the skill. Some players may need to be physically guided through the movements during their first few attempts. For example, some players may need your hands-on help with the throwing motion when they are first learning the skill. Walking unsure athletes through the skill will help them gain confidence to perform the skill on their own.

Your teaching duties don't end when all your athletes have demonstrated that they understand how to perform the skill. In fact, a significant part of your teaching will involve observing closely the trial performances of your players.

As you observe players' efforts in drills and activities, offer positive, corrective feedback in the form of the compliment sandwich described in unit 3. If a player performs the skill properly, acknowledge it and offer praise. Keep in mind that your feedback will have a great influence on your players' motivation to practice and improve their performance.

Remember, too, that young players need individual instruction. So set aside a time before, during, or after practice to give individual help.

What Planning Do I Need to Do?

Beginning coaches often make the mistake of showing up for the first practice with no particular plan in mind. These coaches find that their practices are unorganized, their players are frustrated and inattentive, and the amount and quality of their skill instruction is limited. Planning is essential to successful teaching and coaching. And it doesn't begin on the way to practice!

Preseason Planning

Effective coaches begin planning well before the start of the season. Among the preseason measures that will make the season more enjoyable, successful, and safe for you and your players are the following:

- Familiarize yourself with the sport organization you are involved in, especially its philosophy and goals regarding youth sport.
- Examine the availability of facilities, equipment, instructional aids, and other materials needed for practices and games.
- Find out what fund-raising you and your players will be expected to do, and decide on the best way to meet your goals.

- Make arrangements for any team travel that will be required during the season. Consider clearance forms, supervision, transportation, equipment, contacting parents, and safety.

- Check to see whether you have adequate liability insurance to cover you if one of your players gets hurt (see unit 5). If you don't, get some.

- Establish your coaching priorities regarding having fun, developing players' skills, and winning.

- Select and meet with your assistant coaches to discuss the philosophy, goals, team rules, and plans for the season.

- Register players for the team. Have them complete a player information form and obtain medical clearance forms, if required.

- Institute an injury-prevention program for your players.

- Hold an orientation meeting to inform parents of your background, philosophy, goals, and instructional approach. Also, give a brief overview of the lacrosse rules, terms, and strategies to familiarize parents or guardians with the sport.

You may be surprised at the number of things you should do even before the first practice. But if you address them during the preseason, the season will be much more enjoyable and productive for you and your players.

In-Season Planning

Your choice of activities during the season should be based on whether they will help your players develop physical and mental skills, knowledge of rules and game tactics, sportsmanship, and love for the sport. All of these goals are important, but we'll focus on the skills and tactics of lacrosse to give you an idea of how to itemize your objectives.

Goal Setting

What you plan to do during the season must be reasonable for the maturity and skill level of your players. In terms of lacrosse skills and tactics, you should teach young players the basics and move on to more complex activities only after the players have mastered these easier techniques and strategies.

To begin the season, your instructional goals might include the following for girls' lacrosse:

- Players will be able to maintain possession of the ball, cradle, and dodge.
- Players will be able to throw from the right and left sides.

- Players will be able to throw forehand, backhand, overarm, and under-arm.
- Players will be able to catch on both the right and left sides.
- Players will be able to pick up ground balls from all directions.
- Players will be able to defend an opponent effectively.
- Players will be able to use correct defensive positioning in the midfield and in the arc.
- Players will be able to shoot from both sides of their body.
- Players will be able to intercept and block ball from opponent.
- Players will be able to demonstrate knowledge of rules.
- Players will be able to demonstrate basic offensive and defensive strategies.

For boys' lacrosse, your instructional goals might include the following:

- Players will be able to assume and maintain the "ready" position.
- Players will be able to cradle with either hand.
- Players will be able to throw and catch with both hands.
- Players will be able to shoot correctly with either hand.
- Players will be able to make accurate passes to stationary and moving teammates.
- Players will be able to catch passes while stationary or moving.
- Players will be able to maintain control of the ball while running.
- Players will be able to position themselves and then shuffle their feet to guard an opposing ball carrier.
- Players will be able to cross over and run hip to hip to guard an opponent moving full speed.
- Players will be able to position themselves correctly to guard opponents away from the ball.
- Players will be able to perform correct hold techniques on an opponent moving to the goal.
- Players will demonstrate knowledge of riding and clearing strategies.
- Players will demonstrate knowledge of lacrosse rules.
- Players will demonstrate knowledge of offensive and defensive strategies.

Common goals for both girls' and boys' lacrosse might include these:

- Players will be able to communicate with teammates.
- Players will develop a respect for teamwork.
- Players will show respect for officials, coaches, and other players.
- Players will learn how to win with class and how to lose with grace.

Organizing

After you've defined the skills and tactics you want your players to learn during the season, you can plan how to teach them to your players in practices. But be flexible! If your players are having difficulty learning a skill or tactic, take some extra time until they get the hang of it—even if that means moving back your schedule. After all, if your players are unable to perform the fundamental skills, they'll never execute the more complex skills you have scheduled for them, and they won't have much fun trying.

Still, it helps to have a plan for progressing players through skills during the season. The 4-week sample season plans in appendices A and B show how to schedule your skill instruction in an organized and progressive manner. If this is your first coaching experience, you may wish to follow the plan as it stands. If you have some previous experience, you may want to modify the schedule to better fit the needs of your team.

The way you organize your season may also help your players to develop socially and psychologically. By giving your players responsibility for certain aspects of practices—leading warm-up and stretching activities are common examples—you help players to develop self-esteem and take responsibility for themselves and the team. As you plan your season, consider ways to provide your players with experiences that lead them to steadily improve these skills.

What Makes Up a Good Practice?

A good instructional plan makes practice preparation much easier. Have players work on more important and less difficult goals in early-season practice sessions. And see to it that players master basic skills before moving on to more advanced ones.

It is helpful to establish one goal for each practice, but try to include a variety of activities related to that goal. For example, although your primary objective might be to improve players' scooping skill, you should have players perform several different drills designed to enhance that single skill. To add more variety to your practices, vary the order of the activities you schedule for players to perform.

In general, we recommend that in each of your practices you do the following:

- *Warm up.*
- *Practice previously taught skills.*
- *Teach and practice new skills.*
- *Practice under competitive conditions.*
- *Cool down.*
- *Evaluate.*

Warm Up

As you're checking the roster and announcing the performance goals for the practice, your players should be preparing their bodies for vigorous activity. A 5- to 10-minute period of easy-paced activities, stretching, and calisthenics should be sufficient for youngsters to limber their muscles and reduce the risk of injury.

Practice Previously Taught Skills

Devote part of each practice to having players work on the fundamental skills they already know. But remember, kids like variety. Thus you should organize and modify drills so that everyone is involved and stays interested. Praise and encourage players when you notice improvement, and offer individual assistance to those who need help.

Teach and Practice New Skills

Gradually build on your players' existing skills by giving players something new to practice each session. The proper method for teaching sport skills is described on pages 30-34. Refer to those pages if you have any questions about teaching new skills or if you want to evaluate your teaching approach periodically during the season.

Practice Under Competitive Conditions

Competition among teammates during practices prepares players for actual games and informs young athletes about their abilities relative to their peers. Youngsters also seem to have more fun in competitive activities.

You can create game-like conditions by using competitive drills, modified games, and scrimmages (see units 7, 8, 10, and 11). However, consider the following guidelines before introducing competition into your practices:

- All players should have an equal opportunity to participate.
- Match players by ability and physical maturity.
- Make sure that players can execute fundamental skills before they compete in groups.
- Emphasize performing well, not winning, in every competition.
- Give players room to make mistakes by avoiding constant evaluation of their performances.

Cool Down

Each practice should wind down with a 5- to 10-minute period of light exercise, including jogging, performance of simple skills, and some stretching. The cool-down allows athletes' bodies to return to the resting state and avoid stiffness, and it affords you an opportunity to review the practice.

Evaluate

At the end of practice spend a few minutes with your players reviewing how well the session accomplished the goals you had set. Even if your evaluation is negative, show optimism for future practices and send players off on an upbeat note.

How Do I Put a Practice Together?

Simply knowing the six practice components is not enough. You must also be able to arrange those components into a logical progression and fit them into a time schedule. Now, using your instructional goals as a guide for selecting what skills to have your players work on, try to plan several lacrosse practices you might conduct. The following examples should help you get started.

Girls' Sample Practice Plan

Performance objective. Players will learn how to position themselves on the 8-meter arc, take a shot, and defend a shot for a free position shot.

Component	Time	Activity
Warm up	10 min	Partner passing and catching Stretching
Practice previously taught skills	20 min	Shuttle: passing, ground balls
Teach and practice new skills	25 min	Free position shooting and positioning; free position on 8-meter
Practice under competitive conditions	20 min	Half-field scrimmage
Cool down and evaluate	10 min	Two laps around field Stretching Quick review Reminder about next practice

Boys' Sample Practice Plan

Performance objective. Players will be able to catch and throw the ball on their non-dominant stick side.

Component	Time	Activity
Warm up	10 min	Partner passing and catching Calisthenics
Practice previously taught skills	15 min	Shuttle: passing, ground balls
Teach and practice new skills	25 min	Catching and throwing on nondominant side; diamond passing on dominant and nondominant side
Practice under competitive conditions	25 min	6 v 6 scrimmage
Cool down and evaluate	10 min	Two laps around field Stretching Quick review Reminder about next practice

✔ Summary Checklist

During your lacrosse season, check your planning and teaching skills periodically. As you gain more coaching experience, you should be able to answer "Yes" to each of the following.

When you plan, do you remember to plan for

____ preseason events such as player registration, fund-raising, travel, liability protection, use of facilities, and parent orientation?

____ season goals such as the development of players' physical skills, mental skills, sportsmanship, and enjoyment?

____ practice components such as warm-up, practicing previously taught skills, teaching and practicing new skills, practicing under competitive conditions, cool-down, and evaluation?

When you teach lacrosse skills to your players, do you

____ arrange the players so all can see and hear?

____ introduce the skill clearly and explain its importance?

____ demonstrate the skill properly several times?

____ explain the skill simply and accurately?

____ attend closely to players practicing the skill?

____ offer corrective, positive feedback or praise after observing players' attempts at the skill?

Unit 5

What About Safety?

One of your players appears to break free down the field carrying the ball. But a defender catches up with, and accidentally trips, the goal-bound player. You notice that your player is not getting up from the ground and seems to be in pain. What do you do?

No coach wants to see players get hurt. But injury remains a reality of sport participation; consequently, you must be prepared to provide first aid when injuries occur and to protect yourself against unjustified lawsuits. Fortunately, there are many preventive measures coaches can institute to reduce the risk. This unit will describe how you can

- create the safest possible environment for your players,
- provide emergency first aid to players when they get hurt, and
- protect yourself from injury liability.

How Do I Keep My Players From Getting Hurt?

Injuries may occur because of poor preventive measures. Part of your planning, described in unit 4, should include steps that give your players the best possible chance for injury-free participation. These steps include the following:

- *Preseason physical examination*
- *Nutrition*
- *Physical conditioning*
- *Equipment and facilities inspection*
- *Matching athletes by physical maturity and warning of inherent risks*
- *Proper supervision and record keeping*
- *Providing water breaks*
- *Warm-up and cool-down*

Preseason Physical Examination

In the absence of severe injury or ongoing illness, your players should have a physical examination every two years. If a player has a known complication, a physician's consent should be obtained before participation is allowed. You should also have players' parents or guardians sign a participation agreement form and a release form to allow their children to be treated in case of an emergency.

INFORMED CONSENT FORM

I hereby give my permission for _____ to participate

in _____ during the athletic season beginning in 199____.
Further, I authorize the school to provide emergency treatment of an injury to or
illness of my child if qualified medical personnel consider treatment necessary *and*
perform the treatment. This authorization is granted only if I cannot be reached
and a reasonable effort has been made to do so.

Date _____   Parent or guardian _____

Address _____   Phone ( )_____

Family physician _____   Phone ( )_____

Pre-existing medical conditions (e.g., allergies or chronic illnesses) _____

_____

Other(s) to also contact in case of emergency _____

Relationship to child _____   Phone ( )_____

My child and I are aware that participating in _____
is a potentially hazardous activity. I assume all risks associated with participation
in this sport, including but not limited to falls, contact with other participants, the
effects of the weather, traffic, and other reasonable risk conditions associated with
the sport. All such risks to my child are known and understood by me.

I understand this informed consent form and agree to its conditions on behalf of
my child.

Child's signature _____   Date _____

Parent's signature _____   Date _____

Nutrition

Increasingly, disordered eating and unhealthy dietary habits are affecting
young athletes. Let players and parents know the importance of healthy eating and the dangers that can arise from efforts to lose weight too quickly.
Young lacrosse players need to supply their bodies with the extra energy they
need to keep up with the demands of practices and matches. Ask your director about information that you can pass on to your players and their parents,
and include a discussion of basic, commonsense nutrition in your parent orientation meeting.

Physical Conditioning

Muscles, tendons, and ligaments unaccustomed to vigorous and long-lasting physical activity are prone to injury. Therefore, prepare your athletes to withstand the exertion of playing lacrosse. An effective conditioning program for lacrosse would involve running and other forms of aerobic activity that mimic the stresses of the sport.

Make conditioning drills and activities fun. Include a skill component, such as cradling, to prevent players from becoming bored or looking upon the activity as work. With basic movements, tag and chase games may be easily incorporated into practice or a drill.

Keep in mind, too, that players on your team may respond differently to conditioning activities. Wide-ranging levels of fitness or natural ability might mean that an activity that challenges one child is beyond another's ability to complete safely. The environment is another factor that may affect players' responses to activity. The same workout that was effective on a cool morning might be hazardous to players on a hot, humid afternoon. Similarly, an activity children excel in at sea level might present a risk at higher altitudes. An ideal conditioning program prepares players for the season's demands without neglecting physical and environmental factors that affect their safety.

Equipment and Facilities Inspection

Another way to prevent injuries is to check the quality and fit of all sticks and protective equipment used by your players. Inspect the equipment before you distribute it, after you have assigned it, and daily during the season. For boys' lacrosse, ensure that all players have adequate helmets, gloves, mouth guards, and arm and shoulder pads. For girls' lacrosse, ensure that all players wear their mouth guards at all times. Worn-out, damaged, or outdated equipment must be replaced immediately.

Remember, also, to examine regularly the field on which your players practice and play. Remove hazards, report conditions you cannot remedy, and request maintenance as necessary. If unsafe conditions exist, either make adaptations to avoid risk to your players' safety or stop the practice or match until safe conditions have been restored.

Matching Athletes by Maturity and Warning of Inherent Risks

Children of the same age may differ in height and weight by up to 6 inches and 50 pounds. That's why in contact sports, or sports in which size provides

an advantage, it's essential to match players against opponents of similar size and physical maturity. Such an approach gives smaller, less mature children a better chance to succeed and avoid injury, and provides larger children with more of a challenge.

Matching helps protect you from certain liability concerns. But you also must warn players of the inherent risks involved in playing lacrosse, because "failure to warn" is one of the most successful arguments in lawsuits against coaches. So, thoroughly explain the inherent risks of lacrosse, and make sure each player knows, understands, and appreciates those risks.

The preseason parent orientation meeting is a good opportunity to explain the risks of lacrosse to parents and players. It is also a good occasion on which to have both the players and their parents sign waivers releasing you from liability should an injury occur. Such waivers do not relieve you of responsibility for your players' well-being, but they are recommended by lawyers.

ASEP Fact

The NCAA conducted a six-year survey of men's and women's intercollegiate sports, and women's lacrosse was third best of the 16 sports tracked for fewest practice and game injury occurrences.

Proper Supervision and Record Keeping

When you work with youngsters, your mere presence in the area of play is not enough; you must actively plan and direct team activities and closely observe and evaluate players' participation. You're the watchdog responsible for the players' well-being. So if you notice a player limping or grimacing, give him or her a rest and examine the extent of the injury.

As a coach, you're also required to enforce the rules of the sport, prohibit dangerous horseplay, and hold practices and games only under safe weather conditions. These specific supervisory activities will make the play environment safer for your players and will help protect you from liability if a mishap does occur.

For further protection, keep records of your season plans, practice plans, and players' injuries. Season and practice plans come in handy when you need evidence that players have been taught certain skills, whereas accurate, detailed accident report forms offer protection against unfounded lawsuits. Ask for these forms from the organization to which you belong. And hold onto these records for several years so that an "old lacrosse injury" of a former player doesn't come back to haunt you.

Providing Water Breaks

Encourage players to drink plenty of water before, during, and after practices and games. Because water makes up 45% to 65% of a youngster's body weight and water weighs about a pound per pint, the loss of even a little water can have severe consequences for the body's systems. And it doesn't have to be hot and humid for players to become dehydrated. Nor do players have to feel thirsty; in fact, by the time they are aware of their thirst, they are long overdue for a drink.

Warm-Up and Cool-Down

Although young bodies are generally very limber, they, too, can get tight from inactivity. Therefore, a warm-up period of approximately 10 minutes before each practice is strongly recommended. The warm-up should address each muscle group and get the heart rate elevated in preparation for strenuous activity. Easy running followed by stretching activities is a common sequence.

As practice is winding down, slow players' heart rates with an easy jog or walk. Then arrange for a 5- to 10-minute period of easy stretching at the end of practice to help players avoid stiff muscles and make them less tight before the next practice.

What if One of My Players Gets Hurt?

No matter how good and thorough your prevention program, injuries will occur. When injury does strike, chances are you will be the one in charge. The severity and nature of the injury will determine how actively involved you'll be in treating the injury. But regardless of how seriously a player is hurt, it is your responsibility to know what steps to take. So let's look at how you can provide basic emergency care to your injured athletes.

ASEP Fact

Of all reported women's collegiate-level lacrosse injuries, 1.5% are head injuries and only 0.05% are eye injuries.

Minor Injuries

Although no injury seems minor to the person experiencing it, most injuries are neither life threatening nor severe enough to restrict participation. When such injuries occur, you can take an active role in their initial treatment.

Scrapes and Cuts

When one of your players has an open wound, the first thing you should do is to put on a pair of disposable surgical gloves or some other effective blood barrier. Then follow these four steps:

1. Stop the bleeding by applying direct pressure with a clean dressing to the wound and elevating it. The player may be able to apply this pressure while you put on your gloves. Do not remove the dressing if it becomes soaked with blood. Instead, place an additional dressing on top of the one already in place. If bleeding continues, elevate the injured area above the heart and maintain pressure.

2. Cleanse the wound thoroughly once the bleeding is controlled. A good rinsing with a forceful stream of water, and perhaps light scrubbing with soap, will help prevent infection.

3. Protect the wound with sterile gauze or a bandage. If the player continues to participate, apply protective padding over the injured area.

4. Remove and dispose of gloves carefully to prevent you or anyone else from coming into contact with blood.

For bloody noses not associated with serious facial injury, have the athlete sit and lean slightly forward. Then pinch the player's nostrils shut. If the bleeding continues after several minutes, or if the athlete has a history of nosebleeds, seek medical assistance.

ASEP Fact

You shouldn't let a fear of acquired immune deficiency syndrome (AIDS) stop you from helping a player. On the field you are only at risk if you allow contaminated blood to come in contact with an open wound, so the blood barrier that you wear will protect you from AIDS should one of your players carry this disease. Check with your director or ASEP for more information about protecting yourself and your participants from AIDS.

Strains and Sprains

The physical demands of lacrosse practices and games often result in injury to the muscles or tendons (strains), or to the ligaments (sprains). When your players suffer minor strains or sprains, immediately apply the PRICE method of injury care.

The PRICE Method

P— Protect the athlete and injured body part from further danger or further trauma.

R— Rest the area to avoid further damage and foster healing.

I —Ice the area to reduce swelling and pain.

C— Compress the area by securing an ice bag in place with an elastic wrap.

E— Elevate the injury above heart level to keep the blood from pooling in the area.

Bumps and Bruises

Inevitably, lacrosse players make contact with each other, with sticks, and with the ground. If the force of a body part at impact is great enough, a bump or bruise will result. Many players continue playing with such sore spots, but if the bump or bruise is large and painful, you should act appropriately. Enact the PRICE method for injury care and monitor the injury. If swelling, discoloration, and pain have lessened, the player may resume participation with protective padding; if not, the player should be examined by a physician.

Serious Injuries

Head, neck, and back injuries; fractures; and injuries that cause a player to lose consciousness are among a class of injuries that you cannot, and should not, try to treat yourself. But you should plan for what you'll do if such an injury occurs. Your plan should include the following guidelines for action:

- Obtain the phone number and ensure the availability of nearby emergency care units. Include this information as part of a written emergency plan before the season, and have it with you at every practice and match.

- Assign an assistant coach or another adult the responsibility of knowing the location of the nearest phone and contacting emergency medical help upon your request.
- Ensure that emergency medical information, treatment, and transportation consent forms are available during every practice and match.
- Do not move the injured athlete.
- Calm the injured athlete and keep others away from him or her as much as possible.
- Evaluate whether the athlete's breathing is stopped or irregular, and if necessary, clear the airway with your fingers.
- Administer artificial respiration if breathing is stopped. Administer cardiopulmonary resuscitation (CPR), or have a trained individual administer CPR if the athlete's circulation has stopped.
- Remain with the athlete until medical personnel arrive.

How Do I Protect Myself?

When one of your players is injured, naturally your first concern is his or her well-being. Your feelings for children, after all, are what made you decide to coach. Unfortunately, there is something else that you must consider: Can you be held liable for the injury?

From a legal standpoint, a coach has nine duties to fulfill. We've discussed all but planning (see unit 4) in this unit:

1. Provide a safe environment.

2. Properly plan the activity.

3. Provide adequate and proper equipment.

4. Match or equate athletes.

5. Warn of inherent risks in the sport.

6. Supervise the activity closely.

7. Evaluate athletes for injury or incapacitation.

8. Know emergency procedures and first aid.

9. Keep adequate records.

In addition to fulfilling these nine legal duties, you should check your insurance coverage to make sure your policy will protect you from liability.

Summary Self-Test

Now that you've read how to make your coaching experience safe for your players and yourself, test your knowledge of the material by answering these questions:

1. What are eight injury-prevention measures you can institute to try to keep your players from getting hurt?

2. What is the four-step emergency care process for cuts?

3. What method of treatment is best for minor sprains and strains?

4. What steps can you take to manage serious injuries?

5. What are the nine legal duties of a coach?

What Is Girls' Lacrosse All About?

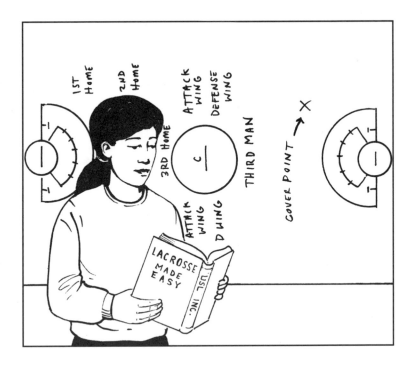

You've probably experienced the excitement of a lacrosse game. Standing on the field 12 meters from the goal, you anxiously await a pass from your teammate. You extend your stick to show where you want to receive the pass, hoping it will be perfectly placed in your crosse. You catch the ball, turn to goal, and focus on the cage. This is the moment you have been waiting for—your chance to score!

Now it's time to share your love of lacrosse with your team. The first part of the book gave you a good, general understanding of what it takes to coach. Now it's time to develop your comprehension of girls' lacrosse. The next three units of *Coaching Youth Lacrosse* provide you with the specific information you will need to teach your players the sport, including basic skills, techniques, tactics, and drills.

Advantages of Lacrosse

You may be less familiar with lacrosse than with some other sports, but lacrosse is a unique game that has many advantages over other activities. Here are some of the reasons we ADVISE youth sport programs to include lacrosse:

A—Able to be played by all ages and levels

D— Develops teamwork

V—Vigorous and continuous exercise

I—Individual skills and challenges

S—Safe, noncontact sport

E—Exciting, unique game

Girls are immediately attracted to the game of lacrosse because it is fast and active. Even though you may not have a vast experience in this sport, you can prepare to teach effectively by using this and other sources. The more enthusiastic you are in your teaching, the more interested your players will be in learning.

How Is the Girls' Game Played?

Girls' lacrosse is a unique combination of individual skills and team performance. Two teams try to score by advancing the ball toward their opponent's goal with a combination of running and passing. The game allows for fast-break opportunities as well as set offensive plays.

A team can't score if it doesn't have the ball, so keeping possession of the ball is integral to the game. The team without the ball plays defense, and it tries to gain possession by intercepting a pass, dislodging a ball from an opponent's stick, retrieving a ground ball, or blocking a pass or shot. When the team gains possession of the ball, it becomes the attacking team and creates a transition to attack the opponent's goal.

All players must develop throwing and catching skills because the ball moves faster through the air than it does when a player runs with it. The objective for the offensive team is to develop a one-on-one or an extra-player advantage (two-on-one) to make scoring easier.

The goalkeeper, who must wear specific protective equipment, defends the goal. When she gains possession of the ball, she initiates the transition to attack. The goal area is defined by a circle with an eight-and-a-half-foot radius, and within that area the goalkeeper has special privileges. Because no one else may enter her crease area, the goalkeeper is unguarded. She may remain in the crease with the ball for up to 10 seconds, and she isn't penalized for using her hands or body to play the ball. When she is out of the goal circle, the goalkeeper has no special privileges and is considered a regular field player.

Girls' and Boys' Lacrosse

The objectives of boys' and girls' lacrosse are the same: Each team tries to control the ball and score on the opponent's goal while preventing the opponent from scoring. The team with the most goals at the end of the game is the winner. Players advance the ball by running with it or throwing it to a teammate. The ball must pass the goal line to score. Given the large playing field, teams and individual players must be prepared to handle offensive, defensive, and transitional situations.

Although the boys' and girls' games share similarities, there are also some major differences. Girls' sticks have a more restricted pocket depth so that the ball is more accessible to the defense, which may only use stick-to-stick contact (the girls' game permits no stick-to-body contact). Boys' sticks have a deeper pocket, which enables players to keep the ball in the stick better. Because of the differences in sticks and pockets, the techniques of throwing, catching, checking, cradling, and shooting differ somewhat in the two games.

In the boys' game, the field markings define the offensive and defensive roles of the players. In the girls' game, players may move freely anywhere on the field. The truly significant difference between the boys' and girls' game is the amount of physical contact allowed, which determines the amount of equipment each player wears.

Age Guidelines

Youth can begin playing lacrosse at any age with modified rules. Younger players will benefit from a game with fewer players so they are more involved in the action. To accommodate the fewer numbers and their lack of physical development, these players should use a smaller field. A regulation field is 100 yards between goals with 10 yards playing space behind each goal. A 50-yard field and five to seven players per team allow maximum activity and involvement for players under age 10. For players age 10 to 13 you may want to shorten the standard field length to 70 to 90 yards between goals. Although it is appropriate to use fewer players on a field this size, we recommend 11 players per team. Continue using modified fields as you teach drills and practice game situations, even after you progress to regulation-size fields for scrimmages.

Manufacturers have developed youth sticks and balls as another way to modify the game for younger players. The modified sticks are not regulation size, they allow for easier catching and throwing, and they are designed to be used with a softer ball. Use a soft foam ball with players age eight and younger. Another way to adapt a stick for early catching and throwing success is to loosen the thongs to permit a deeper pocket. Using a modified pocket is a good starting point, but the sooner you can get your girls playing with a regulation stick the better.

The United States Women's Lacrosse Association's (USWLA) policy is that players under age 13 may not check or have any body contact. The youngest players might start a game with possession instead of with a center draw. With these exceptions, enforce regulation rules to the appropriate level of play. Players can easily adapt all rules and equipment for indoor play. You can replace regulation goals with street hockey goals, indoor lacrosse goals, or even large rubber trash cans.

Allow goalkeepers to defend the goal cage only when they are skilled and are comfortable having shots fired at them. Give individual instruction to a player who desires to play goalkeeper and make sure she's properly equipped before you allow other young players to shoot on her. Players under nine years old should play without goalkeepers unless the keepers are experienced and comfortable in the cage. Shooting nets are good replacements for goalkeepers at any level.

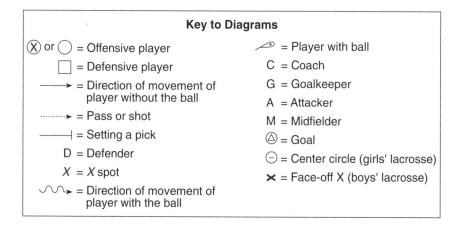

Key to Diagrams	
(X) or ◯ = Offensive player	⌒ᵖ = Player with ball
☐ = Defensive player	C = Coach
⟶ = Direction of movement of player without the ball	G = Goalkeeper
┈┈➤ = Pass or shot	A = Attacker
⟞ = Setting a pick	M = Midfielder
D = Defender	⊘ = Goal
X = X spot	⊖ = Center circle (girls' lacrosse)
⌇⌇➤ = Direction of movement of player with the ball	✕ = Face-off X (boys' lacrosse)

Field Dimensions

One unique aspect of girls' lacrosse is that the playing field has no specific lined boundaries. The field dimensions in girls' lacrosse are defined by natural boundaries—benches, trees, inclines in the ground. Guidelines for field dimensions involve the distance between the goal cages and the amount of playable space behind the goal cages. The amount of playable space behind the goal must be equal at both ends. A second defining trait of girls' lacrosse is that when play stops after a whistle, players must "stand" (remain stationary until play restarts).

As in soccer, field hockey, and ice hockey, play starts in a center circle at the beginning of a game, after goals, and to begin the second half. The goal markings in front of the cage aid in the administration of fouls and penalties (see figure 6.1). A player's starting point on the arc for a free position shot depends on where the foul was committed.

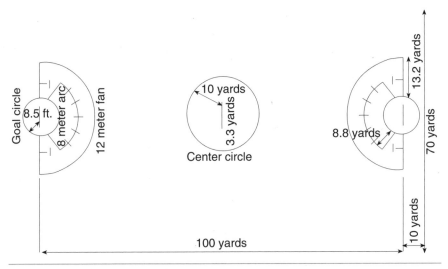

■ **Figure 6.1**   Girls' lacrosse field.

Player Equipment

Young girls need very little equipment to begin to play lacrosse—just a stick, a mouthguard, and a ball. Field players have the option of also using close-fitting gloves, soft headgear, and eye guards or safety goggles that meet American Society for Testing and Materials (ASTM) standards for girls' and women's lacrosse. In some parts of the country, however, safety goggles are a required piece of equipment.

The head of a stick is made from wood or plastic and is then strung with nylon or leather vertical thongs cross-woven with gut or nylon strings. The shaft may be constructed from aluminum, fiberglass, plastic, or wood (see figure 6.2, a-b). In the girls' game, only the goalkeeper's stick may have a mesh pocket (see figure 6.4).

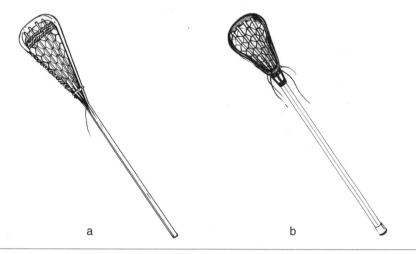

a   b

■ **Figure 6.2**   (a) Wooden stick and (b) molded stick.

The pocket of a women's lacrosse stick is legal if the ball remains even with or above the plastic or wooden walls of the head. See figure 6.3, a-b, for an illustration of a legal and an illegal pocket. At the beginning of every contest, the umpire will check that all players' stick pockets are legal.

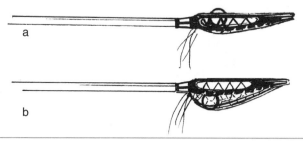

a

b

■ **Figure 6.3**   (a) Legal pocket and (b) illegal pocket.

Regulation sticks are between 35-1/2 and 43-1/4 inches long. However, a beginning player, aged 8 to 10, may play with an even shorter stick (roughly an arm's length). The goalkeeper's stick must also be at least 35-1/2 inches long, but it may be as long as 48 inches. It is composed of the same materials as other players' sticks, and may be strung traditionally or with mesh. The head of the goalkeeper's stick is significantly larger than the heads of other sticks. It measures 13 by 16 inches (see figure 6.4).

■ **Figure 6.4** Goalie stick.

The ball for girls' lacrosse is made of solid yellow rubber, is seven and three-quarters to eight inches in circumference (a little smaller than a tennis ball), and weighs from five to five and one-quarter ounces. Different colors of balls, including white, are available for youth games and practice purposes. Many youth programs use the newly manufactured "soft" ball.

All field players must wear mouth guards. Various sizes are available, so athletes of all ages can find a comfortable mouthpiece that fits correctly.

Unlike field players, goalkeepers must wear protective equipment. They must wear a face mask and helmet, throat protector, and chest protector. Goalkeepers may wear additional padding on hands, arms, legs, shoulders, and chest. Goalkeepers should also wear padded gloves and shin protection, but their protective padding can't be more than one inch thick (see figure 6.5). Manufacturers have recently begun making goalkeeping equipment specifically for girls and are borrowing some ideas from other sports like ice hockey.

Player Positions

A regulation team comprises 11 field players and a goalkeeper. The nature of the game encourages all players to play both offense and defense (there is no midfield division line). Field players are usually categorized as line attack (first home, second home, third home), line defense (point, coverpoint, third man), and midfielders (right and left attack wings, right and left defense wings, and center).

The common characteristics of each position are described next. Remember that these are only guidelines to help you get started fielding a full 12-player team.

Goalkeeper

The goalkeeper's primary job is to defend the goal cage using her stick and her body to prevent the ball from crossing the goal line. The goalkeeper should attempt to save every shot with her stick; her body is a secondary line of defense. To be successful, goalkeepers must develop good footwork, good

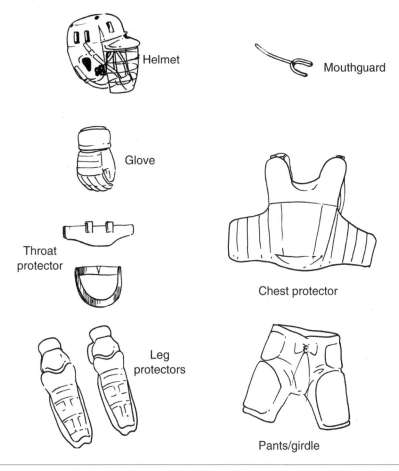

Helmet

Mouthguard

Glove

Throat protector

Chest protector

Leg protectors

Pants/girdle

■ **Figure 6.5**   Goalie equipment.

body positioning, and the ability to cover the angles of shots. The most desirable talents for a keeper are quick reflexes with hands and feet, concentration, and gumption.

Point

The point, as the defender closest to the crease, has duties similar to a sweeper in soccer or field hockey. She has the primary responsibility for individually marking the first home on the attacking team. She must be decisive in evaluating and reacting to the play of her teammates up the field from her. The point should be highly trained to defend the crease, be a reliable stick checker and shot blocker, have strong body-positioning ability, and make good decisions.

Coverpoint

The coverpoint plays in front of the point and is also responsible for individually marking the second home on the attacking team. The coverpoint should be the defender who is most competent in all defensive skills, especially in one-on-one marking ability and body checking, and who, because she leads the defensive unit, is a good decision maker and communicator.

Third Man

The third man usually lines up on the circle for a draw and plays in front of the coverpoint. She is responsible for marking the third home. While still a primary defender, the third man should be assertive in disrupting midfield play by intercepting and sliding to pick up free opponents. When her team has possession of the ball, the third man is often involved in midfield transition and has occasional opportunities to score. The key traits of the third man are blocking skills, ability to anticipate a loose ball and interception opportunities, good timing, instinctive risk taking, speed to recover on defense, and versatility.

Defense Wings

The right and left defense wings mark the opposing attack wings and line up on the circle for the draw. Defense wings need to be the fastest defenders to match the speed of the attack wings and to recover back on defense and pick up a free player. Defense wings, like the third man, must possess good anticipation and marking skills. They must also be good blockers and body checkers. Valuable in transition and opportunistic on attack, defense wings should be capable of shooting from the outside.

Center

The center performs the draw. After the ball is in play, her primary responsibility is to defend her opposing center. If necessary, she fills in for her defensive teammates if they get caught out of position. She is most valuable in transition from defense to offense, and she should possess good field vision and space awareness to serve as a connector. The center must have consistent ball skills. She is a part of both the offensive and defensive units, so she must possess speed and endurance to cover both ends of the field.

Attack Wings

Off the draw, the ball frequently goes to the wings (left or right) who are lined up on the center circle. Attack wings usually are the fastest players who must utilize the space and width of the midfield. Ideally, they use this speed to create a quick transition and lead to a fast break. While in transition, attack wings are called upon to make good decisions about distributing the ball. Often involved in finishing a fast break, attack wings need to be strong passers and shooters.

Third Home

Lining up on the circle, marked by the third man, the third home is a well-rounded attack player with strong ball and shooting skills. She must be able to protect and distribute the ball while in transition to offense. An experienced player, she must be able to anticipate, recognize, and move to open spaces away from the ball to support her teammates. Finding the appropriate spaces allows her many opportunities to score. She should be quick to recognize change of possession and to switch to her defensive role of marking.

Second Home

The second home should be a dynamic attack player with great stick skills. She often is the attack's leader or playmaker. She must be able to get open and receive passes so she can shoot or distribute the ball to her teammates.

First Home

The first home plays closest to the goal and should be able to protect the ball and feed it to her teammates. She must possess excellent cradling, dodging, and shooting skills, be able to react to the ball and her teammates' movement, and have a nose for the goal. In reaction to her opponents' movements, it is to her advantage to be able to cut in limited space and to use the crease.

Umpire

Two or three umpires who know lacrosse enforce the rules to ensure safety, fun, and fairness in the game. An umpire's job is easier when you have emphasized sportsmanship and discipline and have educated players and parents about the rules of the game. The USWLA, which certifies umpires, asks that players, coaches, and umpires observe the intent of the rules and make every effort not to take advantage of them.

Umpires on the field carry a whistle, a yellow flag, and a set of green, yellow, and red cards. The cards are used to control the play and safety of the game and for penalizing poor conduct by the players, coaches, and fans. A green card indicates delay of game and that the next team offense will result in a yellow card. If a player commits a flagrant foul or a dangerous act like slashing or contacting the opponent's head during a check, the umpire issues a yellow card to warn that the next offense of the same nature by the same player will result in her ejection from the game. When a second offense of the same nature occurs, the umpire issues a red card and the player is ejected. Familiarize yourself with the umpires' signals and teach them to the players (see appendix C).

Length of Game

The maximum playing time for a schoolgirls' game is 50 minutes, while collegiate play lasts 60 minutes. Before the game begins, captains or coaches select how long the halftime break will last. It may not exceed 10 minutes. The National Junior Lacrosse Foundation suggests that players ages 10 to 13 play 20-minute halves and players younger than 10 play 15-minute halves. The clock runs continuously during play; it stops only after goals and after every whistle in the last two minutes of each half. If one team leads another by 10 or more goals, the clock keeps running even after a goal is scored. The umpire's signal for illness, accident, or injury also stops the clock.

Starting and Restarting the Game

The captains meet before the game to determine which goal each team will defend. Each half begins with a center draw administered by an umpire. For the draw, two opposing players stand at the center line and place their sticks back to back at or above waist level and parallel to the center line. The umpire places the ball between the sticks. The players and their sticks must remain motionless until the whistle sounds. On the whistle, the players immediately lift their sticks up and away from each other to propel the ball into play (see figure 6.6). The ball must go above head level for play to begin legally. After a score, the umpire restarts play with a center draw.

If the ball goes out of bounds (boundaries are predetermined by the umpires' interpretation of natural boundaries), the umpire blows her whistle to stop play and awards the ball to the player closest to it. All players must move four meters from the boundary, maintaining the same relationship relative to each other as when the ball went out of bounds. The player awarded the ball must be given one meter of free space. Play continues with the official's whistle.

If two opponents are the same distance from the ball when it crosses the boundary or if players commit a double foul, the umpire restarts play with a throw. She positions two players one meter apart, each on the side nearer the goal she is defending. On the whistle, the official throws a short, high lob so that the players take it as they move in toward the game.

Fouls cause game play to stop. When a foul occurs, the official blows her whistle and all players must stand. The next section on fouls explains how to restart a game after a foul.

■ **Figure 6.6**   The center draw: one left hand up and one right hand up.

Fouls

The following section summarizes the most important and influential lacrosse rules. A more thorough review is available in the *USWLA Rulebook* and the USWLA umpiring manual.

Umpires impose a variety of penalties according to whether fouls are major or minor. However, to some extent, the penalty imposed also depends on where the foul occurred on the field. Fouls in the critical scoring area (see Girls' Lacrosse Terms to Know on pages 69-70) carry a different penalty than fouls in the midfield, even if both are of the same magnitude.

Major Fouls

Major fouls are those that are potentially dangerous and that may have a significant effect on the game. Major fouls can be divided into three areas:

1. Fouls involving the stick
2. Fouls involving the body
3. Fouls within the critical scoring area

Fouls involving the stick. If in an attempt to gain possession of the ball a defender uses her stick to slash or check roughly or recklessly, an official will call a penalty. A defender's stick may neither swing toward the body or head of her opponent nor hold her opponent's stick or body. A player with the ball may not hold or cradle the ball in front of her face in an attempt to protect the ball from a defender.

Fouls involving the body. A second category of fouls involves misuse of a player's body. A defender's body must be in position so that she does not reach around the opponent to check the stick, thus the importance of good defensive footwork. A defender may not restrain or hold a player by blocking, detaining, pushing, or tagging an opponent. A player in possession of the ball may not charge, lean into with her shoulder, or back into an opponent.

Illegal pick. An illegal pick is another foul involving the body; it is a major offensive foul. A pick becomes illegal when body contact occurs. A player must set a pick within the other player's visual field, and she must leave enough time or space so the defender can stop or change direction to avoid body contact.

Fouls within the critical scoring area. These three major fouls occur only within the critical scoring area:

1. Three-second violation on a defender. Each defender must be within a stick's reach of her opponent. No defender may stand within the eight-meter arc for more than three seconds without marking an opponent.

2. Obstruction of shooting space by a defender's body. Shooting space is defined as the cone-shaped space extending from the ball to the outsides of the goal circle (see figure 6.7). No defender may stand in or cross through this space when the ball is in the critical scoring area unless her marked opponent leads her into the space. A defender may pass through the shooting space if the player with the ball is not looking to shoot, if the ball is on the ground, or if a pass is in the air.

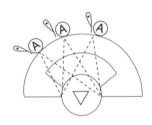

■ **Figure 6.7** Shooting space.

3. A player with the ball who takes a dangerous or uncontrolled shot or has a dangerous follow-through with her stick commits a major foul. The attacker must control the shot and the stick upon releasing the ball. Umpires judge a foul based on distance, placement, and force of the shots. Offensive players may not direct a shot at a field player or the goalkeeper.

When a team commits a major foul in the midfield, the opposing team gets a free position at the location of the foul. The person who committed the foul stands four meters behind the fouled player. In the case of a three-second violation or an uncontrolled shot, the closest player to the girl who committed the foul gets the ball at the free position. All other players must move away four meters in the direction they approached before the official's whistle restarts play.

If the defense fouls within the eight-meter arc, the attack gets the free position from the closest hash mark on the eight-meter arc. The player who committed the foul is placed four meters behind, on the 12-meter fan. The umpire clears the arc (and the penalty lane, if necessary) of all players. The penalty lane is the area four meters, on both sides, away from the fouled player and directly toward the goal. All players must step out of the eight-meter arc toward the closest eight-meter line. This spacing maintains equity of positioning and ensures safety near the goal area. From the eight-meter arc, the player with the ball may shoot directly on goal, pass to a teammate, or run with the ball.

If the attacking team fouls within the eight-meter arc, the defense will get the ball on the eight-meter arc and the attack player who committed the foul must go four meters behind. All players must be four meters away, but players are not cleared out of the eight-meter arc as they are on a defensive foul.

If the major foul occurs in the critical scoring area but outside the eight-meter arc, the umpire awards a free position and repositions players as in a foul at midfield. However, the umpire will clear only the penalty lane to goal.

Minor Fouls

Minor fouls don't jeopardize safety or interrupt play, so the penalties aren't quite as severe. Minor fouls include checking an empty stick and covering or guarding a ground ball with the stick or body. Players who use the hands or body on the ball to gain an advantage, even if the contact is incidental, commit a minor foul. If a player doesn't use a legal stick or a mouthguard or if she wears any jewelry, she commits a minor foul. Other minor fouls include illegal substitution, delay of game, warding off, and intentionally putting the ball out of bounds.

The umpire awards a free position for a minor foul and moves the fouling player four meters away. For a minor foul, the fouling player moves in the same direction that she approached from; in other words, she does not need to go behind the fouled player as she does for a major foul penalty. Again, the umpire's whistle restarts play.

Minor fouls inside the 12-meter fan are penalized with an indirect free position on the nearest spot. The player who committed the foul moves four meters away. The penalty lane is not cleared, and the fouled player is awarded an indirect free position. Indirect free position means the player fouled may not take a shot on goal; she must pass the ball. The umpire awards a free position for minor fouls that are in the critical scoring area.

Play Around the Goal Circle

Specific rules govern play around the goal circle. No player except the goalkeeper or her deputy may enter the goal circle or break the plane of the goal circle at any time. A deputy may enter the goal circle to ensure that she is not hit by a shot only when her team is in possession of the ball and the goalkeeper is out of the crease. Because it alters the game significantly, an illegal deputy results in a major foul. The umpire gives the ball to an attack player on the eight-meter crease and places the illegal deputy four meters behind. The goalkeeper cannot move into the goal circle until play resumes. Like the goalie, a deputy may hold the ball for only 10 seconds while in the goal circle. When inside the goal circle, the goalie may reach outside of her crease to reach a ball with her stick only, but she becomes illegally grounded if any body part touches the ground outside the goal circle.

If the defensive team crosses the line or plane of the goal circle, it commits a minor foul, and the attack gets an indirect free position at the 12-meter arc on either side of the goal and level with the goal line. If an attack player or her stick enters the goal circle, the goalie gets the ball in the goal circle, and all the players must move four meters away before play resumes. A dangerous shot by the attack results in a major foul. The goalkeeper gets the ball and the fouling player must go four meters behind the goal circle.

An official may use a slow, or *held*, whistle under specific circumstances. If the defense commits a foul within the critical scoring area while the attack is on a scoring play and the attack can continue to goal, the umpire throws a yellow flag to indicate the foul. She allows play to continue until the attack loses the ball, shoots, or takes the ball behind the cage for a second time. After one of those events occurs, the official blows her whistle to stop play. The foul is penalized as a major foul within the critical scoring area. The umpire does not use a held whistle for a shooting space violation (see definition on page 70) or any severe foul that causes the ball carrier to come to a stop. Because a defender is at risk of being hit by a shot, the umpire stops play immediately instead of using a flag.

Girls' Lacrosse Terms to Know

arc—Partial semicircle area painted in front of each goal circle at the distance of eight meters and bound by a straight line on the sides that is at a 45-degree angle to the goal line. Used to define three-second violations and in the administration of major fouls.

attack—Players on the offensive team.

backdoor cut—A cut in which the attacking player cuts behind the defender toward the goal or ball.

channel—When a defender forces her opponent to veer in one direction and maintain that path.

critical scoring area—An area on the field, not marked by any lines, with approximate boundaries of 15 yards around and 10 yards behind the goal circle. Used in the evaluation of shooting space.

cut to the ball—An offensive maneuver in which an attack player without the ball runs toward the ball carrier in an attempt to gain a position in front of her defender that enables her to more easily receive a pass.

decoy cut—A cut intended to move the defender out of a space, and not necessarily to receive a pass.

defense—The team not in possession of the ball.

drop down—A defender's move away from her player and toward the goal area to help defend a second player.

fan—A semicircular area painted on the field in front of each goal circle and bounded by a straight line from the goal line extended. Also called the *12-meter arc*, this area is used in the administration of major and minor fouls.

goal circle crease—Home of the goalkeeper, this circle with an eight-and-a-half-foot radius is painted on the field around the goal cage.

goal line—Line painted on the field over which the ball must pass entirely for a team to score a goal.

indirect free position—The result of a minor foul in which the player awarded the ball may not shoot immediately. She must pass the ball to a teammate or wait to shoot until her stick has been checked by a defender.

mark—To defend one particular player, usually within one arm's and stick's length of that player.

off-ball movement—Cuts and picks by players without the ball that cause the defense to relocate.

offense—The team in possession of the ball.

open player—An offensive team member who is not marked and does not possess the ball.

passing lane—The aerial space between the ball carrier and her teammate's stick through which a pass would travel if it were made.

pick—The stationary position established by an offensive player close to the side of the defender with the purpose of allowing another teammate without the ball to lose her defender because the defender must run around the player setting the pick.

penalty lane—An imaginary path to goal defined by two parallel lines that extend from each side of the goal circle to four meters on either side of the fouled player. The umpire clears the lane in some situations when the defense fouls.

player to player—A defensive strategy in which each defender closely marks one opponent and remains with that player throughout the play.

quick stick—A shot in which an attack player receives a pass and takes a shot all in one motion without cradling.

roll—A pivoting move away from a defender and toward the goal or the ball after a player sets a pick or a screen.

roll the crease—A move around the goal circle by an attack player with the object of cutting off her defender on the goal circle and taking a shot on goal from close range.

screen—An offensive tactic in which one player establishes a stationary position close to the side of the defender so that a teammate with the ball may run close to her and force her defender to slow, switch with another defender, or lose her defensive body positioning.

shooting space violation—Foul that occurs when a defender obstructs the free space to goal within the critical scoring area. Free space to goal is defined as an imaginary path from the ball to the outside of the goal circle.

slide—A move by a defender to leave one player to mark a more dangerous opponent.

sphere—Imaginary seven-inch area surrounding a player's head. The ball carrier must keep her crosse and the ball outside of this seven-inch sphere, and the defender may not check into the sphere. She may check through it as long as the check is going away from the head.

strong side—The side of the field that the ball is on.

three-second violation—A violation by a defender who is not marking an attack player but who remains in the eight-meter arc for three seconds.

warding off—Using an arm to push off from a defender.

weak side—The side of the field that the ball is not on.

What Girls' Lacrosse Skills and Drills Should I Teach?

So far, this book has addressed how to teach skills, what skills are necessary for individual positions, how to plan practice, and girls' lacrosse rules. This unit teaches beginner skills and the activities you can use to develop them in your players. Emphasize each of the skills in this unit equally so each player can become complete and well rounded. Lacrosse players, like basketball players, should be taught both offensive and defensive skills. To help you select which drills match the skill level of your players, we've labeled every drill with either a *B* for beginner, *I* for intermediate, or *A* for advanced.

OFFENSIVE SKILLS

Because lacrosse is essentially a giant game of keep-away, individual possession of the ball is integral to the success of the team. Before you introduce team concepts, help individual players become proficient at basic stick skills. Teach players to develop proficiency with both right and left hands for these skills.

Cradling

Cradling is the skill of moving the stick in a semicircular pattern to create a centrifugal force that keeps the ball in the pocket. A player with possession of the ball must cradle the ball to keep it in her stick. All other skills develop from the cradle, so your players should learn this skill first.

Teach players to follow these steps when they are cradling:

1. Grasp the throat of the stick with the dominant throwing hand.
2. Line up the *V* of the dominant hand with the center of the pocket as shown in figure 7.1 (the *V* is the space between the index finger and the thumb).
3. Position the top hand at shoulder height or above.
4. Keep the bottom hand at waist height.
5. Move the stick from one shoulder to the other (see figure 7.2, a-b).
6. Open and close the wrists fluidly to keep the pocket toward the body.

After a player has learned the fundamental movement of the stick and ball, she may develop alternate methods of cradling to better protect the ball from an opponent. She may alter the height, rhythm, and angle of the stick, and she may alter the area around her body in which she cradles, depending on where her body is in relationship to her defender.

■ **Figure 7.1** Proper technique for cradling.

a   b

■ **Figure 7.2** Move the stick from one shoulder to the other.

================================ **Cradling Drills** ================================

Name.   Rock-A-Bye Baby (B)

Purpose.   To learn the motion of cradling

Organization.   Players sit Indian style with a ball and a stick. Show players the proper grip aligning the *V* of the top hand with the open pocket. The other hand is placed halfway down the shaft. Players raise the top hand and extend the stick at a 45-degree angle from the body. Players will rock the baby (ball) in the pocket following a side-to-side motion not more than 12 inches in diameter. Count so that players can establish a rhythm. When players gain control and confidence, increase pace and progress to a more vertical stick position. Encourage unrestricted motion of wrists and arms. Next, limit cradle to one side of the body.

Coaching Points.   Encourage players to try cradling with both hands. Emphasize unified movement of arms. Repeat these progressions daily.

Variation.   To teach running and cradling. Players hold the stick in front of their bodies, hands about six inches apart in the middle of the shaft. Start jogging with big strides. The stick should move to the same side as the lead foot in a shoulder-to-shoulder motion. Progress in speed and move arms wider on the shaft. Limit the cradling to one side of the body.

Name.   Follow the Leader (I)

Purpose.   To learn to cradle

Organization.   Arrange your players in rows, with four to six players a stick's distance apart in each row. Each player has a ball and faces you. Players imitate your cradling motions. Be sure to change sides, heights, and hands.

Coaching Points.   Emphasize good wrist and arm position. Encourage players to watch you making cradling changes and to not look at the ball in their stick.

Variations.   Have players continue cradling while moving into the following positions and gaits: sit, stand, walk, skip, jog, run, sprint.

Head Honcho. Let the head of each line be the leader for the rest of the row for a specific amount of time. Switch leaders.

Mirror Image. Have players face each other in pairs. One leads, and the partner mirrors her cradle.

Name.   Bridge of Sticks (A)

Purpose.   To practice the control of the cradle by pulling the crosse quickly and smoothly

Organization.   This drill requires 11 players. Two lines of five players face each other and hold their sticks over their heads to create a bridge. The bridge of sticks should alternate sides from one line to the opposite side. The sticks should be about one foot apart, leaving enough room for a player to cradle (serpentine-like) through. The player should cradle through the course quickly and smoothly while trying not to drop the ball. The player who ran will replace one of the 10 players holding a stick. The player who was replaced then runs the course.

Coaching Points.   Emphasize that to properly cradle through the course, the player must move her crosse smoothly and quickly.

Variations.   Using the nondominant hand, cradle through the bridge.

Error Detection and Correction for Cradling

Young lacrosse players have difficulty cradling the ball because they do not use their arms in unison, which causes them to lose the ball.

ERROR: Dropping the ball out of the stick while cradling

CORRECTION

1. Have the player move her arms more fluidly in a full, 180-degree, hinge-like motion.
2. Have the player operate her wrists in unison, creating a smooth movement of the stick.
3. Have the player keep her elbows comfortably at her side, not sticking out and not "glued" to the sides of the body.
4. Have the player rotate the trunk and upper body with the movement of her arms.
5. Have the player hold her stick nearly vertical. As players become more advanced, they can vary the position of the stick.

Dodging

Dodging is the sudden change in movement of the stick and ball away from a defender. One may move the stick and body in a variety of ways to get past a defender. Players can suddenly move the stick from side to side, from right hand to left hand (or vice versa), and from high to low. The body can move from side to side, can change speed, or can roll. Keeping the cradle on one side of the body, players may change the heights of the stick from above the head to as low as the waist. The change in heights may be combined with the pull dodge.

Pull Dodge

The pull dodge is a quick stick movement used to change the location of the stick and the ball to fake out a defender. The pull dodge is the most basic and the easiest of all dodges.

To execute a pull dodge, players must develop these skills:

1. Hold the stick in a protected position off the right shoulder as shown in figure 7.3a (left shoulder for left-handed players).
2. Keep both hands on the stick.
3. Pull the stick across the midline of the body to the other shoulder with one strong sweeping motion (see figure 7.3, b-c).

a   b   c

■ **Figure 7.3** Proper technique for the pull dodge.

Roll Dodge

The roll dodge changes the direction of movement of the body and stick to fake out a defender and avoid her check.

Players executing a roll dodge must learn the following skills:

1. Put the stick on the right side of the body as shown in figure 7.4a (for a right-handed player; vice versa for a left-hander).
2. Plant the left foot (or vice versa) and turn so the back is turning toward the defender.
3. Rotate the hips in the direction in which the body is rotating and take a large step out of the pivot.
4. Protect the stick between the shoulders throughout the dodge (see figure 7.4b).
5. Accelerate out of the dodge and try to step in front of the opposing player.

a   b

■ **Figure 7.4**   Proper technique for the roll dodge.

Change-of-Hands Dodge

This dodge is used to change the direction of the stick from one side of the body to the other. It is the most challenging dodge because it requires proficiency in cradling with both hands. The change-of-hands dodge also forces the defender to change sides.

For a change-of-hands dodge, players should follow these instructions:

1. Keep the right hand (if right-handed) at the top of the stick (see figure 7.5a).

2. Pull the stick across the midline of the body to the other shoulder with one strong sweeping motion (see figure 7.5b).

3. Replace the right hand with the left hand on top.

4. Slide the right hand down to the bottom of the stick (see figure 7.5c).

5. Continue cradling.

When the fundamental dodging movements have been mastered, a player may develop combinations of dodges and add fakes to outmaneuver the opponent. For all dodges, the attacking player wants to accelerate out of the dodge to maintain her advantage on the defender.

a   b   c

■ **Figure 7.5** Proper technique for the change-of-hands dodge.

Dodging Drills

Name.   Slalom (B)

Purpose.   To practice various dodges on the move

Organization.   Four to six players stand facing forward in a row five yards from the player in front of them. Only the player in front of them has a ball. You call out the kind of dodge you want the players to execute, and the first player faces her line and weaves in and out of each of her teammates while running and executing dodges toward the end of the line and back to the front (see figure 7.6). When she returns to the front of the line, she hands the ball to another girl, who continues the drill.

Coaching Points.   Make sure the player keeps the cradle going at all times and that both of her hands work together. Remind the dodger to step around each person and back in line as she approaches the next one. Also encourage players to protect the stick with the body as they step past a player and to time the pull of the stick away from the defender.

Variations.

Race Around the Block. Make the drill a race to see who can run the slalom fastest without dropping the ball.

Concentrate. Have the players execute dodges in a specific order; for example, pull right, pull left, roll dodge, change-of-hands dodge.

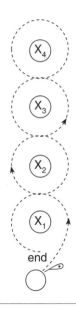

■ **Figure 7.6**   Slalom Drill.

Name.   Grid Dodge (I)

Purpose.   To teach dodging on the move

Organization.   Mark two side-by-side grids, 10 yards by 10 yards, with cones. Place one defender without a stick in each grid. Have the rest of the players line up at one end of the grid, each with a ball behind the first player in line (see figure 7.7). The first player with the ball attempts to dodge the defender in the grid while keeping control of the ball. If she successfully dodged the first defender, she continues on to challenge the defender in the next grid. If she loses control of the ball, she steps out of the grid and gets back in line. If the ball handler dodges both defenders, she continues and shoots on goal.

Coaching Points. Be sure that players move toward the defender and that they time the movement of the stick and body depending on the defender's actions. Be certain that they accelerate around the defender and to the end line. Emphasize protecting the stick from the defender's reach. Be sure that players try all types of dodges and pull to both sides of the body.

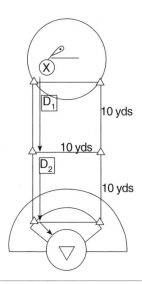

■ **Figure 7.7** Grid Dodge Drill.

Error Detection and Correction for Dodging

As they are learning, players attempt to dodge and they often lose the ball as they go.

ERROR: Ball falls out of the stick while dodging

CORRECTION

1. Have the player move both hands together.
2. Be sure the player maintains a soft top hand on the switch from right to left (or from left to right if left-handed).
3. Have the player continue to cradle on the new side after the strong pull.
4. Make sure that when doing the roll dodge, the player's feet step around the defender and accelerate out of the roll and that she finishes by running forward, not by spinning in place.

Picking Up Ground Balls

Picking up a ground ball is the way players gain possession of a ball while it's moving along the ground. The ball is rarely stationary in a game; however, it is easiest to learn ground ball pickups by practicing on a stationary ball.

When players attempt to pick up a stationary ground ball, make sure they follow these instructions:

1. Bend at the hips and knees (see figure 7.8a).
2. Position the same foot as the top hand next to ball as shown in figure 7.8a (right hand, right foot; left hand, left foot).
3. Accelerate the stick head under and through the ball (see figure 7.8b).
4. Push down with the bottom hand to get the stick vertical.
5. Immediately begin a cradle (see figure 7.8c).

When a ball is rolling away, the player must match the speed of the ball, place the correct foot next to the ball, and execute the same movement as with a stationary ball pick-up.

A ball that is rolling toward a player must be handled differently. Because the player is running toward the ball, she must give with the ball as she does when catching. To take the momentum out of the ball, she reaches toward the ball with the top of her stick touching the ground and the stick angled upward (creating an incline plane). As the ball rolls onto the stick, she gives with the stick toward her body and begins cradling. The player continues cradling as she brings the stick to a vertical, protected position.

When competing with an opponent for the ball, a player positions her body between the ball and her opponent, creating the opportunity for her to play the ball first.

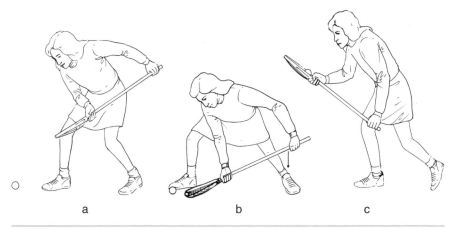

a   b   c

■ **Figure 7.8**   Proper technique for picking up a stationary ground ball.

Ground Ball Drills

Name.   London Bridges (B)

Purpose.   To practice the proper body positioning for a stationary ground ball

Organization.   Arrange your players into pairs and give each pair a ball. Have one player in each pair place the ball beside her foot about 12 inches away. Have her extend her arm from the shoulder over the ball and let her stick hang down toward the ground so that it forms a bridge over the ball. Her partner without the ball starts 10 yards from the bridge and accelerates under the bridge to perform a stationary ground ball pickup (see figure 7.9). As soon as the ball is in the stick, she accelerates and begins a cradle. When she has the ball under control, she drops the ball and sets up a bridge for her partner. Have partners alternate being the bridge and picking up the ball.

Coaching Points.   Emphasize proper body position, especially the foot placement. Be sure the player gets the back of her hands close to the ground and begins a protected cradle as soon as the ball is in the stick. Be sure players accelerate through the ball.

Variation.

Bear at the End of the Bridge. Add a third player (the bear) who is positioned within five yards of the bridge. The player performing the pickup must control the ball right away and dodge the bear. The bear may reach out and try to grasp the ball carrier's stick to dislodge the ball, but she may not move her feet.

■ **Figure 7.9**   London Bridges Drill.

Name.   Scrambles (I)

Purpose.   To teach body position against an opponent before picking up a ground ball

Organization.   Set up two lines of players five yards apart and facing forward. Stand in the middle of the lines with a pile of balls. As you yell the word "Go," roll a ball out away from the players. The first player from each line goes after the ground ball, and the play continues until one of the two players has control.

Coaching Points.   As players accelerate toward the ball, the player closest to the ball should try to step in front of her opponent, using her body to shield the opponent from the ball. Emphasize proper pickup technique and immediate cradle.

Variations.

Ground Ball Toward. Have the players run toward you to practice a ground ball pickup as you roll the ball toward them.

Chance to Score. Stand between the two lines of players and roll a ball away from the players. The player to get control of the ball is the attacker and the other player must play defense all the way to goal.

Ground Ball on the Move. Form two lines facing each other, with three to four players in each line. The first player in one line rolls or bounces a ball across to the first player in the other line, who does a ground ball pickup. The player is to pick up the ground ball and pass it immediately to the next player in line. Then that next player rolls or bounces the ball back to the second player in the first line and the drill continues.

Error Detection and Correction for Picking Up Ground Balls

Beginners often struggle when trying to gain control of a ground ball because they do not position their bodies and sticks correctly. Players lose possession after the ball is in the stick because they do not cradle immediately.

ERROR: Inability to maintain control after picking up a ground ball

CORRECTION

1. Make sure players bend at the hips and knees.
2. Make sure players keep the head over the ball.
3. Have players accelerate through the ground ball pickup.
4. Have players begin cradling as soon as the ball touches the stick.

Throwing

A team can't maintain possession of the ball without good throwing and catching skills. Throwing is propelling the ball from the stick with control. A player can't be a successful passer unless she learns proper throwing technique.

Two styles of overarm throwing are used in girls' lacrosse. The primary style makes use of the strong trunk muscles to aid the throw. In this style, the stick begins the throwing motion from above and behind the shoulder as in pitching a baseball. In the second style, both hands stay on one side of the body and in front of the shoulders. This style utilizes strong wrist snap from both hands. The ball should be thrown and not pushed no matter which style is used.

Players may vary the height of the ball release to provide variety in the throw, resulting in sidearm, underhand, or reverse passes. Players should learn to throw with both the dominant and nondominant hands.

When teaching either style of the overhand throw, make sure your players develop these skills:

1. Pull the stick back and rotate the body to the strong side or top-hand shoulder to prepare for a throw (see figure 7.10a).
2. Slide the top hand so the *V* of the hand is behind the pocket (see figure 7.10a).
3. Position the stick above and behind the shoulder (see figure 7.10a).
4. Move the top hand up first, then toward the target.
5. Snap the wrist.
6. Step onto the foot opposite the throwing hand, then rotate shoulders and trunk (see figure 7.10b).
7. Remember that the path of the stick dictates the direction and path of the throw.

Players will pass to teammates from many angles. At times, a player will pass straight on or face to face because a teammate is making a direct cut. At other times the teammates will be positioned laterally, so a player will pass to the side. In addition to varying the angles at which a pass is made, players need to develop skill in changing the speed and path of the ball. Teach your players to practice hard and soft passes as well as lob and direct passes.

Shovel Pass

The shovel pass is a short lateral or back pass. This pass can be used at any time; however, it is most effective when a player is being double-teamed or cannot execute an overhand pass.

■ **Figure 7.10** Proper technique for the overhand throw.

To perform a shovel pass, a player must follow these steps:

1. Position the stick lateral to the waist, keeping one hand at the butt of the stick and one hand at the throat of the stick (see figure 7.11a).
2. Move the stick in front of the body in a horizontal motion from one hip to the other. Or, move the stick off to the side of the body from in front of the body, at hip level, to behind the body in the shoveling motion. The shoveling motion is similar to the motion used when digging dirt (see figure 7.11b).
3. Follow through until the butt of the stick crosses the opposite hip or is behind the body. The ball is released at the conclusion of the follow-through of the pass (see figure 7.11c).

Lob Pass

The lob pass is a high, looping, over-the-shoulder pass that is difficult to execute. Players should direct a lob pass so that it can be received out in front of the player who will advance the ball.

Instruct your players to lob pass this way:

1. Pull the stick back and rotate the body to the strong side to prepare for the throw.
2. Position the stick above and behind the shoulder.
3. Step with the foot opposite the throwing hand and rotate the shoulders and trunk slightly.
4. Push the top hand forward slightly and slowly release the ball when the stick is almost vertical.

■ **Figure 7.11** Proper technique for the shovel pass.

Throwing Drills

Name. Shuttle (B)

Purpose. To practice accurate throwing and catching

Organization. Place three or four players in a line and have a second line facing them about 15 yards away. The first person in one of the lines has a ball and passes to the first person in the other line. Have players exchange lines after each pass.

Coaching Points. Emphasize all techniques involving proper throwing motion: forward foot is opposite the throwing hand, upper body rotates to prepare to throw, the stick points to target at follow-through. Players receiving the ball should give with the ball or do a wrap catch and go immediately into a cradle. Remind players to catch the ball in front of them and to accelerate through the catch. You can call where to pass from and where to pass to ("Throw high right and catch low left.")

Variations. Change the passes made to include the following:

Long, Short, Short. Player 1, standing in the front of the first line, receives a pass. Player 2, from the second line, runs toward player 1, who passes to her. Player 2 catches, cradles, and passes back to player 1, who is now running toward her. Thus there are three passes made in each trip across.

Error Detection and Correction for Throwing

A common problem for beginners is releasing the ball at the correct time. Many release too late or have poor throwing preparation.

ERROR: The ball is thrown directly to the ground

CORRECTIONS

1. Have the player start the throw with the top hand above and behind the shoulder.
2. Have the player plant the foot opposite the throwing hand forward to allow for trunk and shoulder rotation on the throw.
3. Be sure that the player's bottom arm pulls the butt of the stick toward the body.
4. Be sure all throws involve a wrist snap.

Name.   Four Corners Drill (I/A)

Purpose.   To teach players to make a leading pass to a teammate on the move

Organization.   Make four lines of three or four players each in the corners of a square. The lines should be about 15 yards apart. Player X_1 with the ball begins to jog forward toward another corner line and the first player in that line (X_2) sprints toward the third corner line to receive a leading pass in the middle of the cut (see figure 7.12a). After X_2 catches and gains control of the ball, the player in the third corner line (X_3) sprints toward the fourth corner to receive a leading pass from the second player in the middle of the cut (see figure 7.12b). This pattern is followed around the square as the players concentrate on achieving a high rate of accuracy with catching and throwing leading passes.

Coaching Points.   Emphasize that players should throw the pass out in front of the sprinting teammate so that she must sprint forward to receive the

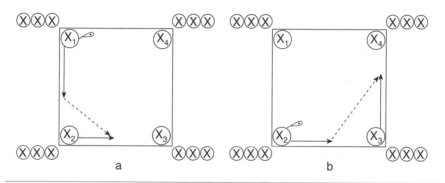

■ **Figure 7.12** Four Corners Drill.

ball. The throwers must make decisions on timing the pass. Instruct the receivers to show a target where they want the ball to be thrown and to accelerate through their cut.

Name. Shoveling (I/A)

Purpose. To practice executing the shovel pass

Organization. Two lines of three players each face each other about 15 yards apart. The first player in the first line has a ball. The first players in each line jog toward each other, and just as they pass one another the player with the ball executes the lateral shovel pass.

Coaching Points. Emphasize proper shovel motion, watching to be sure the stick moves laterally from one hip to the other. Remind receiving players they must be on the strong stick side (the side of the player's dominant hand) or directly behind to receive the pass.

Variation.

Drill Behind Pass. Two players, one with a ball and the other standing about three feet behind, jog the length of the field executing the backward shovel pass. When the player behind receives the shovel pass she can execute the lob pass back to her partner. When they reach the opposite end of the field they can switch roles.

Name. Lollipop Passing (A)

Purpose. To practice executing the lob pass and catch

Organization. Two lines of three or four players each face each other about 15 yards apart. X_1 runs out and passes the ball to X_3 (see figure 7.13a). X_2 begins running out and X_3 throws an over-the-shoulder lob pass to X_2 (see figure 7.13b). X_2 passes the ball to X_5 (see figure 7.13c). X_4 then runs out to receive an over-the-shoulder lob pass (see figure 7.13d). X_4 passes to X_6, and so on. The drill continues until players achieve a high rate of success with the throwing and catching.

Coaching Points. Emphasize all techniques in the proper lob pass throwing motion: foot opposite the throwing hand is forward, the throwing motion stops when the stick is in the vertical position (it doesn't follow through completely). The receiver should receive the ball over the shoulder out in front of her, catching, cradling, and passing.

Catching

Catching is receiving a ball in the air and is largely a skill of eye-hand coordination. Good coordination is most necessary when a player cuts away to receive a pass that requires an over-the-shoulder catch. Players should practice

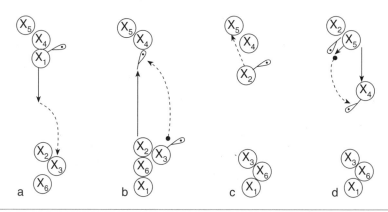

■ **Figure 7.13** Lollipop Passing Drill.

catching the ball from all angles around their bodies, from different heights, and with both hands.

There are two styles of catching. Women, who traditionally used wooden sticks, learned the *wrap catch*. Men, who traditionally used plastic sticks, learned the *give catch*. In the wrap catch, the stick goes to meet the ball. Upon contact, the wrist rotates and wraps the stick around the ball to begin the cradle (see figure 7.14a). In the *give catch*, the stick gives in line the ball (like catching an egg and then giving it back so that it follows the path in which you received it) and then the player begins a cradling motion (see figure 7.14b). Players can use either styles with both wood and plastic sticks. The give catch is easier for young beginning players to understand and execute. The Shuttle Drill on page 86 helps players practice catching.

Teach players the following steps when catching:

1. Watch the ball until it falls into the stick.
2. Extend the arms and the stick to reach for the ball before it arrives.
3. Protect the ball and stick with the body after the catch.
4. Give with the ball as it arrives by softening the top hand momentarily.

Catching Drill

Name.   360-Degree Passing (I)

Purpose.   To learn different points of release when passing and ways to catch the ball from all around the body

Organization.   Place six players in a circle with a diameter of 10 to 20 yards. One player, X_1, stands in the middle of the circle with a ball. The player in the center, who may not move her feet, passes the ball to each player in the circle. The players catch the ball and pass it back (see figure 7.15).

Coaching Points.   Encourage the center player to be creative. She should pass with her wrists from different heights and while rotating her upper

■ **Figure 7.14** The two styles of catching: (a) wrap catch and (b) give catch.

body. Be sure the players are changing hands to throw and catch to gain confidence in passing the ball to teammates who are behind and beside them during play.

Variation.

Whirlwind. As the players improve, have them try the 360-Degree Passing Drill with two balls. This challenges them to concentrate and use their peripheral vision. You can make the drill more challenging by setting a goal of continuing the drill without error for a designated length of time or number of passes.

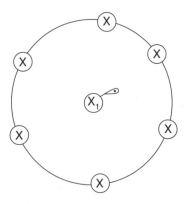

■ **Figure 7.15** 360-Degree Passing Drill.

Error Detection and Correction for Catching

Players, eager to catch the ball, anticipate too much and start to cradle or change direction before the ball is securely in the stick. As a consequence, the ball rebounds off some part of the stick.

ERROR: The ball bounces out of the stick

CORRECTION FOR THE WRAP CATCH

1. Be sure that the pocket of the player's stick is open to the ball before contact and that she does not begin cradling too soon.
2. Be sure that the player extends the stick head before she contacts the ball, and that she does not bat at the ball.

CORRECTION FOR THE GIVE CATCH

1. Have the player maintain a soft grip on the stick to absorb the momentum of the ball.
2. Make sure that the player gives with the ball before cradling.

Shooting

Shooting is propelling the ball toward the goal in an effort to score. Shooting uses the same techniques as throwing, except the ball is directed to a stationary target, the goal. Like passes, shots will come from a variety of release points. Instruct your players to shoot to the open spaces on goal, not at the goalie. Shots taken from a distance require more force, but with all shots, placement of the ball is key. The highest percentage of shots are taken when players shoot in between the goal posts extended. The player should also remember to move the goalie. Once a goalie commits to a head or stick fake, the player can shoot toward the open space.

To obtain accurate placement and increased power on the shot, a player must use a wrist snap. A primary difference between a hard throw and a strong shot is that the strong shot uses a wrist snap to release the ball quickly with added velocity. The wrist should use the same motion to direct the head of the crosse as if the player were releasing a basketball shot or finishing a tennis serve. Both hands work in unison, while the top hand moves back to front and the bottom hand moves front to back.

When players are shooting the ball, be sure they follow these instructions:

1. Position feet toward the goal, with the opposite foot leading.
2. Position hands and shoulders as for a pass.
3. Transfer weight from backward to forward.

4. Follow through in a controlled manner.

5. Control the wrist snap to direct the placement of the ball.

Quick Stick

A quick-stick shot combines eye-hand coordination with the ability to catch the ball and shoot it in one sweeping motion. The quick stick is a very advanced shot and one of the hardest shots to master. It should not be taught to beginning players.

These are skills players must learn to execute a quick stick:

1. Ask for the ball above the head, sliding the top hand slightly down the shaft to extend the stick.

2. Watch the ball into the stick, giving with the hands to get control, but do not start the cradle.

3. When you feel the weight of the ball in your crosse, immediately pull forward and down in one quick motion, snapping the wrists and pointing to a target in the goal.

Bounce Shots

The bounce shot is used to propel the ball down at the ground and thus requires the goalkeeper to make a difficult save.

To perform a bounce shot, players must learn these skills:

1. Bring the crosse back as if to throw, with the opposite foot forward and body ready to rotate.

2. Pull the crosse forward, using more pull on the bottom arm, and snapping the wrists down at the ground.

3. Aim for an area between the crease and the goalkeeper's feet.

Free-Position Shooting

When a defender commits a major foul—blocking shooting space, for instance—within the eight-meter arc, the offensive player gets a free-position shot. All players stop when a whistle is blown. On the eight-meter arc, the offensive player goes to the hash mark closest to where the foul was committed. Those players inside the eight-meter arc must exit the arc at the closest point and stand four meters away from the fouled player. Those players on or outside the arc stand where they are, but must also be four meters from the fouled player.

Several styles can be used to execute a free-position shot. Here is the easiest method for your players to master:

1. Place the foot opposite the throwing arm on the hash mark, turn to the side, and bend slightly at the knees.
2. Hide the sight of the ball from the goalie by resting the crosse on the strong side shoulder and hiding the ball behind the ear.
3. When the whistle sounds, take a slide step forward to gain momentum while pulling the crosse back to shoot.
4. Follow through, snapping the wrists, to the area in the goal where you want the ball to go.

The key to a successful free-position shot is for players to try to move the goalie before they take a shot. To move the goalie, a player can fake with her head or stick. The free-position shot should come quickly after the whistle because defenders will immediately move in to defend the shooter.

Shooting Drills

Name.   Targets (B)

Purpose.   To teach accuracy in shooting

Organization.   Mark the goal into six areas: each of the four corners and two marks in the middle on the sides. Use numbers or colors to indicate each of the areas. Give each player a ball. Divide the group into two lines and position the players one behind the other on the eight-meter arc. Alternating shooting lines, call out an area for the shooter to aim for. Have players step out to the side after they've shot and remain there until all players have shot. All players should retrieve their balls at the same time. Have the shooters practice hitting all six areas from the stationary eight-meter arc mark first and then move to another stationary spot on the arc.

Coaching Points.   From the eight-meter mark, check that the players are planting the foot opposite the throwing arm. Emphasize proper shooting technique, especially the wrist snap.

Variation.

Progression on Shooting. From stationary have players run in to receive a pass, then catch/cradle/shoot, or try executing a quick stick. Two players stand behind the goal (to the right and left) and feed the players who are shooting. You can call the area to shoot toward as the shooter approaches the cage on the run. The shooter may fake to one target and shoot to another.

Name.   Quick Stick (A)

Purpose.   To practice the accuracy of the quick-stick pass and shot

Organization. Place one player (the feeder/passer) behind the goal and a line of girls out just past the 12-meter mark. One at a time, players run in and provide a target for the feeder as she executes a quick stick. The feeder must hit the target for the quick stick to be considered successful. Switch the feeder after one rotation of the line. Players can also enter the arc from different angles.

Coaching Points. Emphasize the one sweeping motion with no cradling. The target must be high and visible.

Variation. Add a defender to the attack line and instruct the offensive player to lose her defender before she asks for the pass.

Name. Bounce Shots (I)

Purpose. To practice the accuracy of bounce shots

Organization. Have several players, each with a ball, stand in a line about two to three feet past the 12-meter line. Place a few targets about two or three feet out in front of the goal. On your call, a player runs in. When she reaches the 12-meter line she starts the bounce shot, aiming for the target you called. Then call a target for the second player on the line.

Coaching Points. Emphasize pulling quickly with the bottom hand, snapping the wrist, and aiming about two to three feet in front of the goal.

Variation. Add a line of defense.

Error Detection and Correction for Shooting

Players often get too excited about shooting on goal and they do not prepare themselves properly for the shot. Often the first thing players see is the goalkeeper and that is the target at which they shoot. Have players look to the spaces around the goalkeeper as targets to aim for, and then shoot.

ERROR: Shooting at the goalkeeper's stick or directly at the goalie

CORRECTION

1. Have players face the cage and look for shooting opportunities.
2. Have players prepare body and stick for release of a shot.
3. Have players shoot for open spaces in the cage.
4. Have players follow through to the target with a strong wrist snap.

DEFENSIVE SKILLS

Defenders guard offensive players to prevent them from scoring. Defenders should try to *mark*, or guard, the player to whom they are assigned, staying near that offensive player and between the ball and the goal. From this position, defensive players will be able to gain possession of the ball with a block, stick check, or pass interception.

Checking

When an opponent has possession of the ball, the defender tries to dictate the path the attacker takes. The defender may choose to force the attacker to her nondominant side, into a double-team, or away from the center of the field where she has many shooting or passing options. The defender does this by occupying the space on the side of the offensive player. When the defender has her body and stick in position, she may perform stick checks in which she tries to hit her opponent's stick to dislodge the ball or interrupt the cradle.

Body Checking

In body checking, the defender moves in the same direction as the ball carrier with her body positioned to deny a space for the ball carrier to use.

Teach players to follow these steps when they body check (see figure 7.16):

1. Keep the feet facing in the same direction as the ball carrier's feet.
2. Remain hip to hip while running with the opponent. Keep body positioned next to the opponent instead of in front of the opponent.
3. Force the opponent to cradle her stick on her weak, or nondominant, side.
4. Strive to control an opponent's path by getting in to a space before the attacker does.

Because so many players rely on the dominant hand for accurate passing and shooting, the defender, by positioning her body as an obstacle on the strong side of the ball carrier, can effectively slow the attacker or force a bad pass. If a defender gets caught on the weak side of her opponent, she should try to cross to the strong side, forcing her opponent to use her nondominant side. This is called *turning*, or *crossing*, a player.

■ **Figure 7.16** Proper technique for body checking.

Body Checking Drill

Name. Crossing the English Channel (B)

Purpose. To practice body checking, footwork, and body position

Organization. Mark off a space about 10 yards by 20 yards with cones or lines. Put players in pairs, give one player (the attacker) a ball. The second player (the defender) has no stick. The attacker runs through the 20-yard channel while the defender tries to maintain proper body position and work on footwork while moving with the ball carrier. The defender should try to remain on only one side of the ball carrier for the length of the channel.

Coaching Points. Use cue words, including "hip to hip," "feet facing forward," or "force her weak." Players should be ready to adjust to the ball carrier's changes of speed and should not let the ball carrier get more than two steps ahead. Maintain a safe distance—about one to two feet—between players so there is space and time to react to movements.

Variation (I).

Meet Me Halfway. Have the defender start halfway across the channel. On the word "Go," the defender tries to close the gap between herself and the ball while trying to get to a side of the channel to force the oncoming ball carrier to her weak side. The defender's footwork timing is critical to success. After players older than 13 have learned proper body position, you can add stick checking.

Error Detection and Correction for Body Checking

Too often, defensive players commit to play the ball for a block or stick check and lose proper body position.

ERROR: Defender loses body position on the ball carrier

CORRECTION

1. Make sure that the defender stays hip to hip and does not get ahead of or in front of the attacker.

2. If the player loses body positioning, she should sprint ahead of the ball carrier and force the ball carrier to cradle on her weak side. This strategy keeps the ball carrier from being able to get a strong shot or pass off.

3. Teach defenders how to block a pass or shot from the proper defensive body checking position. If a player loses body positioning, an alternative is to intercept the ball.

4. Have the defense start on the wrong side of the attacker and learn how to turn or cross the player to develop confidence to control an attacker's movement.

Stick Checking

Stick checking is the repeated tapping motion a defender uses to dislodge the ball from her opponent's stick. All checks must be controlled. We do not recommend stick checking for players younger than 13.

When teaching stick checking, make sure your players have learned the following:

1. Position the body before attempting to stick check.

2. Establish a rhythm and make contact when the opponent's stick is most available. Only stick-to-stick contact is allowed (see figure 7.17).

3. Keep the body in balance for multiple checks.

4. Repeat quick taps and releases on the stick.

Young lacrosse players can become overzealous with stick checks. You must emphasize the importance of body positioning! Injuries occur when players are out of position or are out of control with their stick checks. Immediately penalize illegal stick checks.

■ **Figure 7.17** Proper technique for stick checking.

Stick Checking Drills

Name. Woody Woodpecker (B)

Purpose. To teach the motion and control of stick checking

Organization. Have players stand in pairs. Have one player hold her stick out horizontal to the ground—anywhere from hip to shoulder level—while the second player (a defender) performs a series of tapping motions with the side or wall of her stick, making firm, rapid, and repeated contact (like a woodpecker). Have the defender check downward, upward, and toward (poking) five times each. Have the players switch roles and repeat the series.

Coaching Points. Encourage players to maintain control in their checks. They should use a firm wrist snap and release, which will help them learn to check without a large windup. Repeat the series with a ball and discuss the success of dislodging the ball based on where stick contact is made. Encourage players to practice with both the left hand and the right hand on top.

Name. One, Two, Three, Check (B)

Purpose. To practice footwork and stick checking on the move

Organization. Players line up next to each other in pairs, one a defender and one an attacker. Use no ball at first. Maintaining good defensive body position, players walk across the field as the defender looks for a chance to check the attacker's stick while she cradles. The defender must count out loud each time she sees the attacker's stick available to check. She must reach the count of three before she may make stick contact. (The defender will count "One, two, three," and then will check the next time she sees the stick.) Switch roles when the players reach the other side of the field.

Coaching Points. Encourage the defensive players to watch the attacker's stick and catch the rhythm of the cradle before she attempts stick-to-stick contact. Teach players to be patient and to maintain good body position when they check. Watch for defenders who commit their feet and attempt only one big, swinging check. As players' skills progress, let them do the drill at a jog and then a full run as you add a ball to be checked.

Error Detection and Correction for Stick Checking

A defensive player attempts a one-time swing to check the ball, and if unsuccessful gets beaten by the ball carrier.

ERROR: Defensive player committing to one big swing with her stick

CORRECTION

1. Have the player maintain hip-to-hip body positioning while checking.
2. Have the player stay with the attacker. Do not allow her to step toward the ball to check.
3. Have the player keep her feet moving at all times to position for a check.
4. Make certain the player's checks are small taps.
5. Make sure the player times the stick check with the cradling motion to allow repeated stick-to-stick contact.

Blocking

Blocking is a skill that requires eye tracking and visual coordination; it can be taught. To execute a block, a defensive player positions her stick to block a pass or shot as it leaves the offensive player's stick. Stick position and timing are essential elements of this skill.

Teach your players the following steps to blocking:

1. Extend the stick vertically. Don't reach toward the opponent's stick.
2. Loosen the grip of the top hand and slide the stick through to extend the reach into the path of the ball (see figure 7.18).
3. Let the ball carrier begin the throwing motion before you extend your stick into the passing lane. Timing is critical.

■ **Figure 7.18** Proper technique for blocking.

Blocking Drill

Name. Monkey in the Middle (B/I)

Purpose. To practice the skill of blocking

Organization. Player 1 and player 2 stand facing each other 10 yards apart. As player 1 passes the ball to player 2, a defender (the "monkey") stands one step in front of player 1 and attempts to block the pass. If the monkey is successful, she gets possession and carries the ball to the other end. If she is unsuccessful, she must circle player 1 and sprint to the other end where she tries to block player 2's shot, who now passes to player 1. Have passers and monkeys alternate roles after a certain time.

Coaching Points. Reinforce the key points of the skill. Be sure players do not leave their feet and jump to try to block the pass. Success comes with practice in learning to watch the ball and quickening the stick slide through the hands.

Variation.

Heighten the Challenge. To increase the level of challenge, make these adjustments: Allow the passers to fake. Move them farther apart. Let them pivot on only one foot and protect the ball before the pass, making it more difficult for the monkey to see the ball. Use two monkeys, one at either end.

Intercepting

Intercepting is catching a pass that was intended for the opponent. Interceptions are a matter of timing, anticipation, and patience. Intercepting is one of the hardest skills to master, but it is valuable in game situations.

Have your players follow these instructions to execute an interception (see figure 7.19):

1. Extend the stick.
2. Reach beyond the opponent's stick.
3. Time the stick's acceleration into the passing lane.
4. Beat the opponent to the ball.

■ **Figure 7.19** Proper technique for executing an interception.

Intercepting Drill

Name. Cougars on the Chase (B/I)

Purpose. To teach tracking, timing, and anticipation on interceptions

Organization. Player 1 and player 2 stand 15 yards or more from each other and pass one ball back and forth. A line of three or four players stands five yards to the side and at right angles to players 1 and 2. As the ball leaves the stick of player 1, a player standing to the side of player 2 accelerates into the space in front and tries to intercept the pass. If she intercepts the pass, she returns the ball to player 2 and runs to the end of the line by player 1. If she doesn't intercept the pass, she returns to the end of the line that she came from. Passers change at some point as well.

Coaching Points. Interceptors have to be catlike in their anticipation and reaction to the ball in the air. Encourage the "cougars" to sprint and then reach for the ball with a fully extended stick. Also have the cougars reach and step toward the ball as they go to catch it. Change the side and angle of approach of the interceptors to include starting from behind the passers.

Detection and Correction for Blocking and Intercepting

Blocking and intercepting both rely on patience, timing, and good visual tracking. When the defender senses the ball is about to be released, she should track the ball into her stick for the block or interception. Defensive players, in their eagerness to get the ball, often commit with their sticks and bodies too soon.

ERROR: Missing the ball in flight

CORRECTION

1. Have players keep sticks in ready position and extend them at the proper time. Do not let them swing the sticks in the air in an attempt to bat the ball.

2. Have players extend their sticks straight up for the block. Do not allow them to step or reach forward toward the opponent.

3. Have players keep eyes on the ball, track it, and see it into their sticks.

4. Have players extend their sticks beyond the opponent's for an interception and accelerate through the catch.

Defensive Positioning

Individual defensive positioning refers to the defensive player's position in relation to the ball *and* to an opponent without the ball. In the instructions on body checking, you learned about the importance of the defender's body positioning in relation to the ball carrier. If a defender's opponent does not have possession of the ball, she must adjust her position in relation to her opponent and the location of the ball. The closer the ball carrier is to her teammate, the tighter the defender should mark her player. If the ball carrier is far away, she can take a step or two away from her player (without the ball) so she can see her player and the ball carrier with enough space and time to make an interception.

These are the key points to emphasize in teaching defensive positioning (see figure 7.20):

1. Position yourself so you are closer than your opponent to both the goal and the ball.
2. Keep your stick up to show you are covering the passing lane and are ready to intercept.
3. See both the ball carrier and the player you are defending at all times.
4. You should constantly be repositioning as the ball is passed or carried to a new location.

When defending within the arc, a defender wants to deny the strong cut, catch, or side shot. If her player is behind the goal, she should position herself so she can see both the ball and her opponent. She must also be aware of specific rules concerning defense in the eight-meter arc.

■ **Figure 7.20** Proper technique for defensive positioning.

Defensive Positioning Drills

Name. Half Field One Versus One (I)

Purpose. To practice body positioning and forcing an opponent to her weak side

Organization. One line of players, each player with a ball, stands at the bottom of the center circle facing the goal. A second line of players (defenders) stands just off to the right of the 12-meter fan. (If a player is left-handed the defender will start on the left side of the 12-meter fan). The first person in each line moves forward for one-on-one play. As the player with the ball starts down the field, the defender tries to create an open lane toward her opponent's weak (nonstick) side by blocking the lane to the stick side. The defender should make herself appear as big as possible by holding her crosse in one hand and her other arm extended over her head to form a *V*. As the attacker gets closer, the defender's feet should begin moving with the attacker. When the opponent is within a stick's length, the defender brings her crosse in, holds it with both hands, and mirrors her opponent's crosse. Keeping her feet moving, a defender should try to stay on her opponent's weak shoulder, about half a step ahead, and between her opponent and the goal.

Coaching Points. Emphasize the defender's making the weak side lane appear open, keeping feet moving, and remaining between the opponent and the goal.

Name. Freeze Pass (B)

Purpose. To teach defensive positioning in relation to the ball and a goal

Organization. Four to six pairs of players scatter around the 12-meter line. One player in each pair has a pinnie to designate her a defensive player. Offensive players may not move from their spots as they pass the ball among each other. Offensive players hold a caught pass until you have a chance to check the defensive position of each defender. You then blow your whistle so the attacker may make another pass. Defenders may not intercept or block the passes. They should concentrate only on moving their feet and sticks into the proper area in relation to the ball and their opponents.

Coaching Points. Review the position of each defender as each pass is made. The player on the ball should adjust to force the ball to the attacker's weak side. Players next to the ball or one pass away should step up so their sticks are in the passing lane. Defenders off the ball should adjust their positions so the passer, the receiver, and the defender are forming a triangle. The defender should be positioned between the passer and the receiver and be forcing the opponent to catch the ball on her weak side.

Variation.

Midfield Area. Using the same organization, position the players in the midfield around the center circle or wider on the field to show how large a triangular space defenders can cover while preparing to cover on the weak side of the field.

Error Detection and Correction for Defensive Positioning

A defender off the ball often makes two common mistakes: She watches the ball as she cuts and loses track of her player, or she watches only her player and is not aware of where the ball is.

ERROR: Allowing the opposing player to get away or losing sight of the ball

CORRECTION

1. Teach players to always see and know where both their marked player and the ball are.
2. Teach players to anticipate opponents' cuts and not to only react to them. Players should always stay between their opponents and the goal.
3. Teach players to anticipate an overthrow or loose-ball situation and encourage them to get to the loose ball first.

As a team develops defensively as a unit, a defensive player must know when to leave her assigned player and help a teammate. To make this decision, a defensive player must evaluate whether her marked opponent being unguarded is more dangerous than threat of the ball carrier's scoring. She must therefore know where both the ball and her opponent are located to make a good decision. Proper defensive positioning is critical to the development of a team defense.

How Do I Get My Girls to Play as a Team?

After your team has practiced the individual skills, you may introduce team tactics that involve more players and act as the building blocks for team development. You must teach both offensive and defensive tactics to all players, because lacrosse is a game of transition.

The most effective way to teach these team principles is with small-sided drills and games. Using fewer players and a smaller space allows you to organize specific ball and player movement and to reinforce one tactic at a time.

What About Team Offense?

As in all games involving a ball, it is faster to move the ball in the air than by running. Moving the ball through the air requires you to teach passing and cutting as well as player and ball movement principles. Every time a player catches the ball, she needs to turn to goal and challenge the defender to make herself a scoring threat.

A team with possession of the ball has two objectives: to move the ball down the field and score and to maintain possession of the ball so the opponents cannot score. The following offensive teamwork concepts will help a team accomplish these objectives.

By catching the opponents in a slow transition to defense, the attacking team can often create an excellent scoring possibility. Each time a team gains possession of the ball, the players should look for opportunities to create a fast-break or extra-player situation. If these efforts do not result in a quick attack shot or goal, the team must have at least one basic offensive movement pattern designed to create other good scoring opportunities.

Moving to Get the Ball

A player must first move to get away from a defender so she has some free space in which to catch the ball and receive a pass from teammates. This maneuver is best accomplished by making a smaller move or step to get the defender on the wrong foot or by moving in the wrong direction. Such individual maneuvers are similar to basketball moves, with common names like *jab step, stutter step, crossover, roll,* or *change of direction*. When the defender has been outmaneuvered, the attack player accelerates, or *cuts*, into a space.

Players may cut in all directions in relation to the ball. The most difficult to defend is a cut directly to the ball, where the attack player has gained a step on the defender and positions her body in front of the defender to protect her catch. However, space and a defender's position may require a cut in a different direction, such as away from the ball or flat (90 degree). For instance, it's a flat cut if you run straight across the width of the field when the ball is coming straight down the length of the field. Often a player cuts for the ball and runs out of space on the field or gets too close to the ball carrier. You must also teach players how to make space on the field for themselves or their teammates. Making space refers to the act of clearing an area for a player to cut into to receive a pass.

Error Detection and Correction for Moving to Get the Ball

Often the attacker simply attempts to outsprint the defender and is not free to receive a pass. When she continues the cut too long she gets too close to the ball carrier.

ERROR: Cutter is not free to receive the pass from her teammate in time to use the existing available space

CORRECTION

1. Encourage the attacker to learn many different moves to cause the defender to misstep, and then to spring to the ball.
2. Teach the attacker to make an adequate space to cut into before she accelerates into the ball.
3. Teach the attacker to get a step ahead of the defender, then to step across the defender's path to use her own body to protect the catch.

Space and Timing of Cuts

When a player masters the skill of freeing herself to receive a pass from a teammate, you can begin to develop the concept of teamwork—consecutive passes among teammates to maintain possession while advancing the ball along the field. While attacker 1 is cutting to receive a pass from player 2, attacker 3 is preparing to cut to receive a pass from player 1. Teach all beginning lacrosse players the concepts of making space to cut into and knowing the proper timing of a cut.

All young athletes find the skills of making space and knowing when to use this space challenging. Most young athletes move into the space where they want to catch the pass, then they stand and scream for the ball. They have used up the space in which they want to catch the ball too soon and they stop, which often results in an opportunity for a defender to intercept the pass. A player must first decide if there is enough room around the ball to cut into, and then decide when to cut. Players learn how to make these decisions through trial and error in drills. The Count Up Passing Drill on page 114 provides situations to learn the proper decisions of space and time.

Supporting the Ball

Knowing when and where to cut are some of the most important and challenging decisions for each player on the field. The player with the ball should have three passing options: She should be able to pass the ball forward, laterally, or backward (a *backpass*). Passing the ball forward toward the goal advances the ball most directly and is most threatening to the defense. A lateral pass across the field is appropriate to get the ball to a part of the field that has more open space and to a player who may not be so closely marked. A backpass allows a team time to reposition itself, to create and use space, and also possibly to change sides of the field. To support the ball after each pass, players off the ball need to constantly move to reposition themselves so that the player with the ball has all three options available. Backpasses are often made to the goalkeeper because she is an unmarked player who can use her goal circle for protection.

To move the ball in all directions, every player must be able to throw and catch on all sides of her body while being guarded by a defender. A player who cuts to receive a pass may be open for only a brief moment; therefore, the passer must always be ready to release the ball to a teammate.

Error Detection and Correction for Supporting the Ball

If a pass is incomplete, the failure could lie with either the passer or the cutter. Often, a ball carrier has tunnel vision toward the goal and is unlikely to look for options to her side or behind her. A passer must keep her stick in a ready position to pass the ball at any moment and in any direction. A cutter may fail to provide support to the passer at the right time; she moves too early or too late into a space. All teammates should try to be aware of each other so that two cutters do not cut into the same space at the same time.

ERROR: The passer was not able to deliver a pass to her teammate

CORRECTION

1. Teach players with the ball to look and listen for teammates in all directions around them for an opportunity to pass.

2. Make sure the player with the ball is ready to release a pass in an instant when she locates a free teammate.

3. Encourage attackers to give several options to the ball carrier by cutting into several different spaces around her.

4. Encourage attackers to be aware of their teammates and not just the ball so they do not all cut into the same space at the same time.

Spreading the Attack

All team games that use a ball make using space properly a challenge. Offensive players must keep reasonable distances between each other and the ball to create space for teammates to pass into, run through, and move the ball efficiently in. When attackers bunch up, the defenders are brought too close together, which makes it easy for them to check, double-team, block, or intercept the ball. When two attack players stand very near each other, one defender can guard both.

Girls' lacrosse has no offside rule to prohibit the movement of the attack players in relation to their goal area. Therefore, it is sound attacking strategy to position some attack players close to the goal so they may cut to the ball and then sprint downfield to get in a position (lower) between the goal and the ball carrier. The cut, replacement below the ball, and recut process allows players to use, create, and reuse the space in front of goal. When teaching a player to create space for herself or another teammate, instruct her to not cross in front of the ball carrier. The ball carrier, then, retains the option to go to goal herself.

Setting Picks

Players use a pick to help a teammate get free to cut to the ball. Two teammates come close together to try to gain an advantage for one of them. The pick is accomplished by the players physically blocking a space so the defender must take extra steps to get around the opponent (see figure 8.1). The block allows an attacker to gain a step or two advantage on the defender. A

■ **Figure 8.1** To set a pick, one player physically blocks a space so a defender must take extra steps to get to her opponent.

pick must be set to the side or within the visual field of the opponent—giving her enough time and space to stop or change direction.

Playing Behind the Goal Circle

A unique aspect of girls' lacrosse is that the ball and any of the players are allowed to use the space behind the goal circle. Space behind the goal circle provides a great area in which to feed the ball to a teammate. A direct feed for an immediate shot, like you might see in ice hockey, is the most challenging play for goalkeepers to defend. It is also very difficult for the goalkeeper and the defenders to cover the ball behind the crease while paying attention to movement and cutters in front of the goal. As the offense changes the point of attack by moving the ball to behind the cage, defenders often have to reposition. During this adjustment, an alert attacker can cut free to the cage. That's because taking the ball behind leaves the attacking team with a chance to settle the ball without one-on-one defensive pressure and to organize into an offensive pattern of play.

Teach young players how to feed a pass from behind the cage to a teammate in good scoring position. A player with the ball behind the cage has almost unlimited space and time to look for a feed to a teammate; however, her pass will have to avoid the goal cage and goalkeeper, and she must send it accurately and time it correctly. Encourage the feeders to raise their sticks up so they release the ball from a position above the goal cage. Figure 8.2 illustrates a traditional behind-the-goal setup.

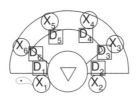

■ **Figure 8.2** Traditional behind-the-goal setup.

Offense in the Critical Scoring Area

An attacking team should have a plan for organized movement when it has advanced the ball to the critical scoring area (see figure 8.3) and no fast-break or extra-player situation has developed. Often a team will initiate such a play or movement pattern from behind the goal because there is less defensive pressure.

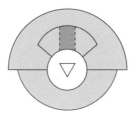

■ **Figure 8.3** The critical scoring area.

Many offensive plays and patterns may be effective in creating a scoring opportunity, and they can be easily borrowed from other team sports like basketball, ice hockey, water polo, or soccer. Some examples appropriate for youth may include these concepts:

- **Pass and cutaway.** After a pass to a teammate who is around the 12-meter line, the passer cuts backdoor to catch her defense watching the ball, not the player. The cutaway also leaves space for the player with the ball to challenge to goal. A second pass and cutaway strategy is for a player to pass the ball to another teammate behind the goal and then to set a pick on the opposite side of the arc so a teammate may cut to the ball.
- **Priority cuts toward the ball and in front of the goal cage.** With every pass, a player from the opposite side of the arc should cut directly to the ball through the primary scoring area in front of goal, asking for the ball. The feeder should first look to pass to these cuts. If a pass to them would be unsuccessful, she should look next to her other options.

- **Use two passes to move the defense, then look to the opposite side of the field for an opening.**   Make at least two consecutive passes in the same direction (to the right or to the left), which will cause the defense to shift in that direction. While the ball is being passed in one direction, two players on the opposite side of the 12-meter fan set a pick. The attacker using the pick cuts across the eight-meter arc toward the ball, followed by her teammate, who set the pick.
- **Double two-player stack at the 12-meter arc.**   Set up with two feeders behind the cage, one on each side, and place two stacks of two people on the 12-meter arc. As the ball is passed to one of the feeders behind the cage, the two players in the stack opposite from the feeder work together to set picks for each other, and these players cut to the ball as a first and second cutter.

Offensive Team Drills

Name.   Post Drill (B)

Purpose.   To teach offensive skills of cutting and getting free while practicing individual defensive positioning and intercepting

Organization.   Arrange players in groups of three with one ball. Designate one player as the passer, feeder, or "post." The other two players are designated as attack and defense. For a series of six passes in a row, the attacker uses different moves to get free from the defender and cuts to catch the pass from the post. She must make space for herself to cut into between each pass by moving away from the post in any direction. The defender pressures each catch and practices marking and intercepting. The ball returns to the post after each attempt.

Coaching Points.   Require the attacker to use different individual moves to get free for each of the six passes. Encourage the attacker to use different-sized spaces around the post to cut into. Make sure the attacker asks for the ball away from the defender. The defender should practice marking the attacker closely and going for interceptions.

Variations.

Double Post. Add another post 20 yards away from the first post. The posts should face each other. Require the attacker to catch from one direction and pass the ball to the new post, simulating a pass down the field. Specify which cuts are allowed. For example, cuts can be made only toward the ball, not away from it. If the defender can't intercept the ball, encourage her to position her body to force the attacker's weak side; add blocking skills later. You can also add blockers to the post position so the post must feed under more pressure.

Consecutive Feed and Shot. Position six feeders, each with a ball, outside the 12-meter arc (including behind the cage on an extended goal line). Position an attacker inside the eight-meter at a center point with a defender covering her. The feeders take turns feeding the attacker. The attacker tries to get free to catch the pass, but she must stay within the 12-meter arc. The drill simulates a game because feeders must be ready at all times to pass with limited space. The attacker's stick may be available to receive for only a second. With each successful catch, the attacker should shoot at the cage. Defenders work on marking closely, intercepting, and blocking the shot. Defenders over age 13 may also practice checking.

For beginners, number the feeders from one to six and have them feed in numerical order. For intermediate players, allow any feeder to make the pass. Be sure the feeder makes eye contact with the attacker before she makes the pass. With advanced players, challenge feeders by putting defenders on them who are permitted only to block.

Name.   Pass Along (I)

Purpose.   To teach the elements of spacing and timing on cuts to the ball

Organization.   Space six players in a row, each player approximately 10 to 20 yards from her neighbor and facing forward (see figure 8.4). The first player in line (X_1) has a ball. X_1 rolls the ball forward on the ground, picks it up, then turns and accelerates toward X_2. X_2, meanwhile, has been moving off the ball in any direction (pretending to lose defense) during X_1's ground ball pickup. X_2 establishes eye contact with X_1, then cuts at speed to receive the ball. X_3 begins moving while the ball is in the air to X_2. Play continues down the line in this manner. After X_1 passes, she sprints to the end of the line to take her place behind X_6. If she can beat the ball to the last player in line, she can add in. If the ball progresses faster than X_1 does, X_6, upon receiving the ball, throws a long pass to the new top of the line. The second player in line becomes the new head of the line and the process of passing down the line continues.

Coaching Points.   Emphasize preparing before a cut and cutting at speed to the ball. Be sure the receiver changes directions after the catch and accelerates toward the next player in line. All players must see the ball so they are ready to react to an overthrow or missed catch. This drill emphasizes that if the ball is caught and thrown accurately, it moves faster than a runner.

Name.   Count Up Passing (A)

Purpose.   To teach players to support the ball and make space ahead of time for quick ball movement

Organization.   Start with one team, either offensive or defensive, of four to six players in a 20-by-20-yard playing area (see figure 8.5). Assign each member of the team a number. Designate a specific amount of time for the first round. As round 1 opens, X_1 starts by passing the ball to X_2, who passes to X_3, and so on in order. All players must be in constant motion as they work to get free from their defense and cut to receive the ball. The team is awarded a point if every player has caught the ball in succession before the

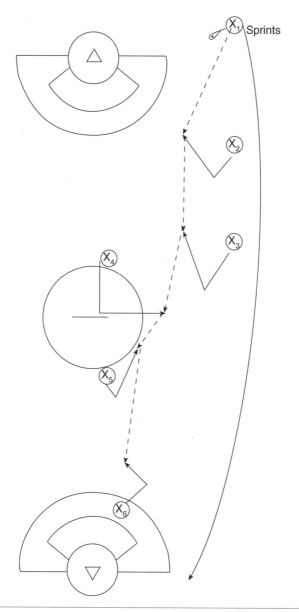

■ **Figure 8.4** Pass Along Drill.

allotted time is up. You can then put an offensive and a defensive team in the 20-by-20-yard playing area and have them perform the drill. Teams can also switch roles—offense becomes defense and defense becomes offense—as round 2 begins. Teams can compete to see which one has the higher score at the end of the drill.

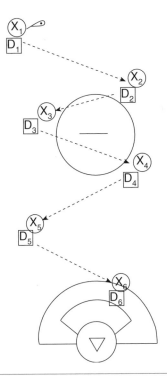

■ **Figure 8.5** Count Up Passing Drill.

Coaching Points. This drill, like Pass Along, teaches players how to move off the ball and position themselves to cut to the ball. The main difference here is that in a confined space players must keep moving to create space for their teammates. Players must plan ahead to move in relation to the moving ball. The added defense requires players to get free from a defender. You can incorporate a transition factor so that when defense gets possession it immediately starts its passing up series.

Variations.

Teambuilding (B). Don't require a passing order. Instead, require that all players must touch the ball (but not in a specified order) before the team scores a point.

Space and cutting (I). Require the cutter to move in a certain direction to the ball carrier before she can make a pass. For example, she can cut only toward, only away, or only flat.

Challenge (A). Add a defensive player for each offensive player to increase the difficulty of getting free and catching under pressure. Repeat the progression of variations: counting up, each player touching, and specified types of cuts.

Transition. When the defensive team intercepts the ball, it should begin its sequence of passes, continuing in order "around the horn." For example, on a five-member team, if X_4 intercepts a pass, she automatically passes to X_5 on her team, who passes to X_1, who passes to X_2, and so on. Only when the team has passed through the order is a point scored.

Name.   Magnet Tag (I)

Purpose.   To teach space awareness to young players

Organization.   Spread four to six players out in a 20-yard-square space. One player is "It" and wears a yellow pinnie. Half of the remaining players wear red pinnies, and the other half wear green pinnies. All players with red pinnies have a negative charge and players with green pinnies have a positive charge. Players must stay at least five yards away from other players with their same-colored pinnies (like charges repel each other). Players may be close to other players wearing different-colored pinnies (opposite charges attract). If a player is touched by "It" or is caught within five yards of a player with a same-colored pinnie, she becomes neutral and must stand and do 10 jumping jacks or other exercises. Change the "It" after a designated period of time.

Coaching Points.   Look for players who are too close to players with same-colored pinnies and identify them as neutral. Keep reminding the players that they must be aware of "It" and of keeping a distance from their teammates. This drill helps players develop spatial awareness between themselves and the ball or other players.

Name.   Pass and Set a Pick (A)

Purpose.   To practice setting legal picks off the ball for a teammate

Organization.   Divide the players into groups of four with one player, a defender, wearing a different-colored pinnie than the others (see figure 8.6). One attacker has the ball. The defender guards one of the attackers who doesn't have the ball. A second attacker sets a pick for her guarded teammate. If the pick was set correctly, the guarded attacker should be able to get free from the defender to receive a pass from the player with the ball.

Coaching Points.   First watch the player setting the pick to be sure it is a legal pick. Then change your focus to the player who is using the pick. Encourage this player to pass close by her teammate and continue directly to the ball. Switch the defensive player after each player has set a pick two times.

Variation.

Option 2. Another way to set up this drill is to have player 1 approach the defender and position herself stationary and to one side of the defender. (Blind or back picks are illegal in lacrosse). Player 2 should cut off the closest shoulder of the player setting the pick and accelerate to the ball to receive a pass. After the feeder has passed, she positions herself to set a pick for player 2, who is now being guarded by the defender.

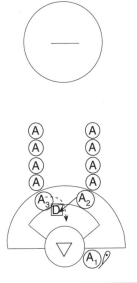

■ Figure 8.6 Pass and Set a Pick Drill.

Name. Feeding Frenzy (A)

Purpose. To practice feeding while guarded from behind the goal

Organization. Set up two lines of shooters at the 12-meter arc (see figure 8.7). Position one feeder (X_1) behind the crease and off to one side, with extra balls lying safely in the back of the crease. Place one defender (D_1) on the goal line extended who attempts to block the feeder's pass. Be sure the defender stays off to the feeding side and does not creep to the middle, because each feed should result in a shot on the goal cage. One player from each line cuts toward the cage for a feed. If a player catches the feed, she may shoot for the goal right away. Cutters return to the end of the opposite line, and the feeder prepares for the next pair of shooters. The drill continues until X_1 has used all the balls. Gather the balls, and X_2 becomes the next feeder.

Coaching Points. Help the feeder decide where and when to feed cutters. Remind her to keep her stick up and to use her wrist to snap the feed. She must learn to feed around the defender's stick and to not always telegraph where she is feeding. The cutters should always move in some other direction before cutting to receive a feed at full speed. An experienced goalkeeper could be added to cover the space over the crease; however, she will face very challenging shots from unmarked shooters at close range, so use good judgment.

Variations.

Offensive Pairs. Have both shooters work together before cutting. Encourage them to cross over in their paths to goal. More advanced players may set a pick and roll off to the goal.

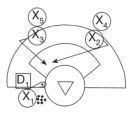

■ **Figure 8.7** Feeding Frenzy Drill.

Defender's Decision. Allow one defender to chose which shooter she will cover and be sure the defender gets correct body position on the cutter. The feeder should read the situation and feed to the unmarked cutter.

Name. Three by Three-Second Drill (A)

Purpose. To help an offensive unit around the goal cage move in relation to each other and to score off a feed

Organization. Four to six attack players spread out around the 12-meter arc and behind the goal cage. After a player passes the ball to a teammate, the group has three seconds to accomplish three things: 1) The two players who are most directly opposite the ball cut through the eight-meter arc looking for a feed. 2) The noncutting players move to fill any gaps the two cutters made and to balance the rest of the unit. 3) All players must complete their moves, clear the arc, and set back up within the three seconds and then be ready to receive the next pass. The goal of the drill is to keep the ball moving continuously.

Coaching Points. This drill helps young attack players develop a sense of movement toward and around the ball as they take turns being cutters and feeders. Reward players who make good cutting decisions and those who clear the eight-meter arc quickly. When a player receives a pass, she should look to feed and not look to pass right away. In this drill you feed to someone who can shoot and pass to someone who can restart the cutting sequence or change the position of the ball. Be sure players use the space behind the goal cage.

Variations. Vary the time limits and number of cutters. Add a few marking defenders and allow players to feed to unmarked attackers for shots. Eventually add full team defense.

Special Offensive Situations

Play stoppage sets up most special situations. Teach your players the specific advantages and disadvantages of these situations.

Free Position on the Eight-Meter Arc

After a major foul in the eight-meter arc, the official designates the fouled player or another player to take a position, with the ball in her stick, on a hash mark on the eight-meter arc. All other players must clear the eight-meter arc to the closest point four meters away from X_1 (see figure 8.8). D_1 must go four meters behind X_1. The player may shoot, pass, or run with the ball when the whistle sounds. Many players run into the eight-meter arc to try to get closer for a shot, but this often leads to a successful block or stick check by a defender and a loss of possession for the attacker. A better option is to pass to a teammate who is in better position to shoot or who is behind the goal and can challenge or reset a play. Although a player may shoot right off the whistle, youth players often lack strength and physical development to shoot successfully from the eight-meter. However, shooters may use a bounce shot, which is difficult for a goalkeeper to handle, especially if the ground is uneven.

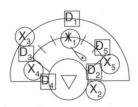

■ **Figure 8.8** Free position on the eight-meter arc.

Free Position on the 12-Meter Arc

After a minor foul by the defense in the 12-meter arc, the official awards the offense an indirect free position on the 12-meter arc. The player with the ball may not shoot on goal, so she should pass the ball to a teammate who may be free to shoot right away. If moving the ball closer to the goal is not a good option, then she should create space by cradling or running the ball away from the goal and then passing to a teammate.

What About Team Defense?

The best team defense is a pressuring player-to-player marking system in which players are also trained to help each other. The best way to defend as a unit is to be interdependent and interacting. Teammates help each other by constantly communicating about the location of the ball and the position of players in an attempt to create a turnover by surprising and pressuring the player with the ball.

Double-Team

A double-team occurs when two defenders simultaneously commit to defend the ball carrier with the purpose of checking the stick and gaining possession of the ball. One defender forces the ball carrier to cradle on one side so that a second defender can read the situation and add in (see figure 8.9). A double-team should allow one of the defenders to stick check while the other defender maintains solid body checking position. By increasing the pressure on the ball, defense creates the opportunity for a turnover or forces the ball carrier to give up possession.

When a defender prepares to leave her opponent to double-team, she calls "Double" so her teammates know she has left a player open. When her teammates hear she is leaving to double-team, they act as a unit to cover for her and mark the open player. This is called a *defensive slide* or *sliding to the open player*.

A double-team can be used successfully anywhere on the field. However, if the ball carrier outmaneuvers the two committed defenders or passes to the free player, the defensive team risks chasing the ball down the field. This may result in an offensive fast-break or extra-player opportunity. Double-teams must be well executed and well timed, or the call to double may turn into a call for trouble.

Crease Defense

The crease defender is a player who defends an opponent who is behind the goal line extended. (We recommend that defenders at the youth level not follow

■ **Figure 8.9** Positioning for a double team.

their girl behind the cage.) When she is in position in front of the cage, the defender must make sure that she is in a legal and safe playing position. The defender's mission is to take the space ahead of the ball carrier and to move out to guard a player and prevent a drive to the cage. The crease defender may not be in the shooting lane, commit a three-second violation, or enter the goal circle. When she is defending a player with the ball who is challenging from behind the cage, she should meet the player just behind the goal line extended and then force her up the side of the eight-meter fan (see figure 8.10). She always tries to keep her opponent moving away from the cage and to continually decrease her angle for shooting. This situation is often a good time for a double-team.

Defending a Pick

Teammates must communicate to successfully defend against picks. When a defender realizes that her player is going to set a pick, she must tell her teammate where the pick is coming from. She must then allow space between her and her player for her teammate to pass through. Only in emergency situations—when there isn't enough space, for example—should teammates switch players on a pick.

Defending a Fast Break

If the attacking team gains a numerical player advantage when coming through the midfield, the defensive unit downfield must prepare to meet the chal-

Error Detection and Correction for Crease Defense

Far too often, an attacker who challenges a defender from behind the crease is able to outrun the defender and turn the corner toward the middle of the field and take a high-percentage shot.

ERROR: The offensive player is able to shoot from the middle of the field after challenging from behind the crease

CORRECTION

1. Remind defenders that their job is to limit or dictate where the offensive player may go with the ball.

2. Review and encourage defenders to concentrate on proper body checking and footwork, and then, if in position, to consider a stick check or a block.

3. Encourage the defender to lead the attacker where she wants her to go instead of following her.

4. Practice the timing of a defender getting to the goal line extended, planting a foot to push off, and changing directions before the ball carrier arrives (see figure 8.10).

■ **Figure 8.10**   A crease defender's proper body and stick positioning determine the path an attacker follows.

lenge of being outnumbered and to prevent a high-percentage or an unguarded shot. The defense should pressure the ball as soon as possible to slow the attacker's progress down the field, while the weak-side and lower defenders recover below the ball and evaluate how to best prepare for defensive coverage. With the objective of buying as much time as possible to allow more teammates to move downfield, defenders attempt to slow the ball's movement by constantly reacting to the ball movement and communicating with each other about who is pressuring the ball and who is covering. The goalkeeper should think of herself as the last defender, and she should go out of her crease to intercept passes as necessary rather than letting a free attack player catch a feed and shoot on her.

Defensive Transition From Goalkeeper Clear

After the defensive team has gained possession of the ball, it must have a strategy for clearing the ball out of the defensive end of the field. It is often helpful to pass the ball to the goalkeeper when organizing a transition, because she may hold it in the goal circle for 10 seconds. The organization for transition begins with creating space on the field so that players may cut back to the ball. The goalkeeper clears to a side, not directly in front of her, because a turnover in front provides an opportunity for an instant shot on her goal. Additionally, after the ball has been cleared, a weak-side defender recovers to a position in the center of the field to act as a safety valve in case of a turnover farther up field. The new offense supports the ball with three options at all times, with players in position to receive a back, lateral, or forward pass.

▪▬▬▬▬▬▬▬▬ Defensive Team Drills ▬▬▬▬▬▪

Name. Channel Escort (A)

Purpose. To teach defenders to move together and to communicate while forming a double-team

Organization. Mark a channel 10 yards by 20 yards with cones. Arrange players in groups of three with one ball per group. Player 1 has the ball and stands at the short end of the channel. Player 2, without a stick, stands next to her in good defensive body-checking position. Player 3, also without a stick, stands five yards down the channel. When player 1 begins to move the ball, player 3 tells player 2 she is in position and will add on to double-team player 1. Player 3 then positions herself correctly, and the two defenders maintain this relationship for the full length of the channel. Switch defenders' roles to come back up the channel. A different player becomes the ball carrier after each round trip.

Coaching Points. Encourage loud, crisp verbal signals. Stop the play to correct the defenders if they are out of position. Show players how to recover if the ball carrier gets to the outside of either defender. The second defender (player 3) may start from different positions in the channel.

Name.   Double Trouble (I)

Purpose.   To teach defenders when to stay with their girl and when to help a teammate double-team the ball

Organization.   Create two teams of two players each and give one pair pinnies. Have the attacking pair start with the ball outside of the 12-meter arc, while each of the defenders marks her assigned attacker. Have the foursome play two-on-two to goal, and continue play until the attackers turn the ball over or shoot.

Coaching Points.   Encourage defenders to make decisions about when to stay with their players and when to help a teammate by double-teaming. The attempted double-team will at times be unsuccessful (the attacker will make her pass), and in those cases the defender should return to her original player. Emphasize communication and decisive action by the defense. This drill provides a good time to reinforce the offensive tactics of making space to cut into and keeping a distance from teammates, and it requires the defense to make a commitment to a double-team.

Variations.

Above and Below. Have the ball carrier and her defender start in the midfield while the other pair starts nearer to goal. Then start the pair with the ball closer to the goal than the pair without the ball. These changes affect the defensive team's decisions and actions. Start the ball behind the crease to practice crease defense and the possible opportunities to double-team a player challenging around the crease. The changing ball locations give players a chance to practice realistic game scenarios.

Defensive Advantage. Add an extra defender who double-teams the ball whenever it is in the 12-meter arc. Increase the number of players on each team, up to six-on-six with an extra defender, to help players make decisions involving sliding and covering within the defensive team.

Name.   Sole Survivor (I)

Purpose.   To practice one-on-one defense and offense around the crease

Organization.   Assign half your players to be attackers and the other half to be defenders. Each of the attackers has a ball and positions herself behind and off to the side of the cage. Each defender waits in line outside the top of the eight-meter arc. Players challenge each other one-on-one, with the attacker coming from behind the crease to challenge on either side. Play ends when a foul occurs, a shot is taken, or a turnover occurs. If the offensive player scores, the defender joins the attack line. If the offensive player does not score, she joins the defense line. Play continues with repeated one-on-one challenges until no players remain in one of the lines.

Coaching Points.   Emphasize defensive footwork in playing an attacker coming from around the back of the crease. Support defenders who allow the attacker to shoot only from low angles or far from the goal. Set a time limit, such as 10 seconds, for the attacker to shoot. It is also helpful to use a shooting net or a goalkeeper to help defenders.

Name.   Introduction to Transition (Three-on-Two, Two-on-One) (I)

Purpose.   To teach players to react to a turnover both offensively and defensively and to practice an extra-player offensive situation

Organization.   Place two goals about 40 yards apart. Send two players to defend one end, and divide the remaining players into three attacking lines at the other end (see figure 8.11). One player from each attack line moves out and the attackers move the ball downfield toward the goal and try to score on the defenders at the other end. If the attackers get a successful shot off, their turn has ended and the next three attackers in line begin the drill. If the defenders cause a turnover, the two defenders make a transition to attack and try to bring the ball down to the opposite end goal. The three original attackers must now play defense on the two transitioning players. If the ball is brought to the other end by the defense or if a goal is scored, play ends.

Coaching Points.   This is an excellent drill to get players to react to changing possession and switching back and forth from attack to defense. Encourage the two defenders to communicate about who is marking the ball and who is covering, which will alternate frequently given that this is a three-on-two. That's why communication is so important. The attackers must pass accurately and keep space between them so a single defender can't cover two players. Movement off the ball is also a key to offensive success.

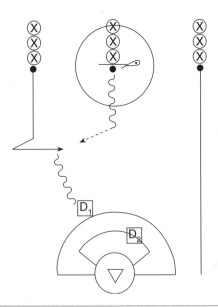

■ **Figure 8.11**   Setup for the Three-on-Two Drill.

Name.   Half-Field Situations (I)

Purpose.   To teach the offense how to take advantage of an extra-player, fast-break situation and to teach the defense how to handle the same

Organization.   Set up four attackers, three defenders, and one ball as shown in figure 8.12. The ball starts on the outside midfield. Start play and continue until there is a turnover or a shot on goal. Reset the players back in midfield with a new ball. For example, A_1 wants to make a defender (D_1 or D_2) commit to her. When one or both defenders commit, then A_1 can pass to her open teammate.

Coaching Points.   Freeze the play to illustrate to a player both good and questionable decisions. Watch for defenders who make decisions too early or too late in relation to the ball movement, and note those who make no commitment or who don't communicate when they make a move. Most attackers will run with the ball for too long before passing to an open teammate. Have the attackers keep an appropriate distance from other attackers and move the ball quickly with accurate passes to the free player so the defenders are the players who move the most.

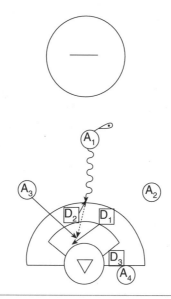

■ **Figure 8.12**   Setup for the Half-Field Situations Drill.

Ways to Scrimmage

Establishing gamelike scenarios and special conditions are beneficial ways to scrimmage. Small-sided games allow for maximum player participation and coaching feedback. It doesn't matter how many players are on the field, as long as you emphasize the rules and concepts of the game of lacrosse.

Restrict players with the ball to encourage players to pass the ball more and run the ball less. Not allowing players to hold the ball for more than 5 seconds and requiring the player with the ball to stop running and to pass immediately are conditions that increase passing. These restrictions also require players off the ball to think ahead and to get into good position to cut in support of the ball because the ball progresses more quickly downfield through the air. You can add another condition: Every player on the team must touch the ball before a shot to help distribute the ball and to prevent two or three players from dominating play.

Another way to develop awareness of offensive or defensive concepts is to place conditions on the ball's movement on the field. You can add conditions like requiring a "give and go" or a back pass before a shot to any small-sided game. A give and go is when one player passes to a teammate and sprints ahead (to lose her defense) to get an immediate pass back from her teammate. You might also require the ball to cross over to the other side of the field through the center circle before a shot can be taken. The crossover strategy helps ensure that players remain balanced on both sides of the field and are aware of the available spaces on the weak side.

Lacrosse is unique in the way it allows players to use the space behind the goal. An effective way to teach new players to use this space is to require them to take the ball behind the cage at least one time before they take a shot on goal. Another way to encourage play from behind the cage is to require that all shots be fed from a pass that comes from behind the goal line.

Extra-player situations occur often in a game, and every player should learn how to deal with the situation, whether her team is the one with or without the extra player. Controlled, small-sided games using a neutral player to add to the attack or defense on each possession is a good way to practice fast-break transition situations and to encourage double-teams.

You can play many popular games with their normal rules using lacrosse equipment. Such favorites as baseball, basketball, ultimate Frisbee, steal the bacon, and many others are good games to use to help young players practice lacrosse skills while playing a game they probably already know.

Practice Games

Name. Half-Court Lacrosse (A)

Purpose. To practice quick transition near a goal with teams playing both offense and defense

Organization. This game is played within 15 meters of the goal, with only three players per team. Start play by throwing the ball between any two opponents. When a team gains possession, it tries to score. Should a turnover occur, the defensive team must pass or run the ball anywhere outside of the 12-meter arc before it may go on the attack. All fouls are administered as a minor, indirect free position at the 12-meter arc. Play for five minutes or until one team scores five goals. When a team scores, it gets possession at the 12-meter arc ("make it, take it").

Coaching Points. Most young players understand the drill easily when you describe it as similar to half-court basketball. Encourage players to switch quickly from defense to offense and back again. Be creative. Any previously mentioned ball or player restrictions may be added.

Name. Ultimate Lacrosse (I/A)

Purpose. To emphasize the need for supportive cuts to advance the ball

Organization. This game can be played with any size field and any number of players. The player with the ball may not run with it; she may pivot to find free space in which to pass. The defender on the ball must be one stick's distance away and may only block, intercept, or recover a ground ball. She may not stick check.

Coaching Points. This game emphasizes passing and cutting quickly before the defense can apply pressure. All offensive players must think about positioning—not only for the first cut to the ball, but also to find space not occupied by a teammate for cuts after one or two passes. Defensive players must concentrate on maintaining proper midfield positioning to intercept and blocking passes from stationary players.

Name. Four-on-Four Plus One (I/A)

Purpose. To work on principles of offense and defense, and specifically on taking advantage on attack and learning to slide on defense when outnumbered

Organization. This game should be played on a smaller field (goals 40 yards apart) and should include a goalie. One free player is always on attack.

Coaching Points. Emphasize creating an extra-player situation on attack as well as learning to defend when outnumbered. Remind the offense to spread the defense and to move the ball with passes. Remind the defense to communicate and to slide as the ball is passed. You may add restrictions such as requiring everyone on offense to touch the ball before a shot or having a "give and go" pass accompany each new possession.

Name. Four-on-Two Continuous (I/A)

Purpose. To teach the goalkeepers to look for and execute a quick clear to the side of the field to create a fast-break transition and scoring opportunity

Organization. Play this game on a smaller field (two goal cages 40 to 50 yards apart). Place a goalkeeper in each cage with an extra supply of balls. Position two permanent defenders who will stay at each end of the field

$(D_1, D_2, D_3,$ and $D_4)$. Two lines of players are set up at midfield and the two players who are first in line $(X_1$ and $X_2)$ will be attacking players, positioned by the starting goalkeeper. These attacking players need to be ready to join in on the first clear only. Play starts when one goalkeeper passes to one of the attacking players in the midfield lines (see figure 8.13a). The two players who started by the goalkeeper and the two midfielders $(X_3$ and $X_4)$

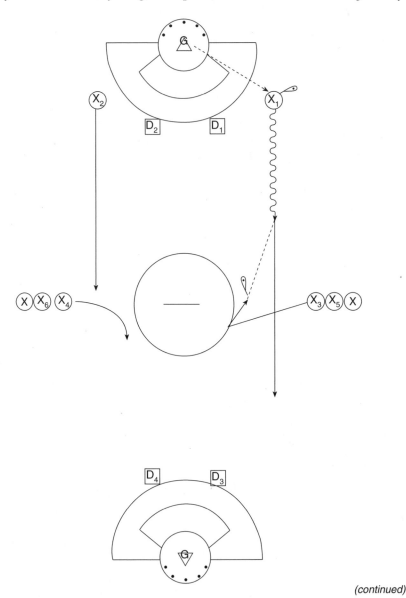

(continued)

■ **Figure 8.13a** Four-on-Two Continuous Drill.

join the receiver. These players move the ball among themselves as they attack the far goal against the two defenders, D_3 and D_4. Upon a turnover or any shot (see figure 8.13b), the defending goalkeeper clears to the midfield (X_3 or X_4), and two new midfielders (X_5 and X_6) run to add in at the other end. After a midfielder has been on attack at both ends she is finished, and she adds to the back of the midfield lines to await her next turn.

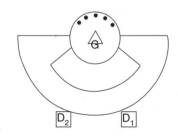

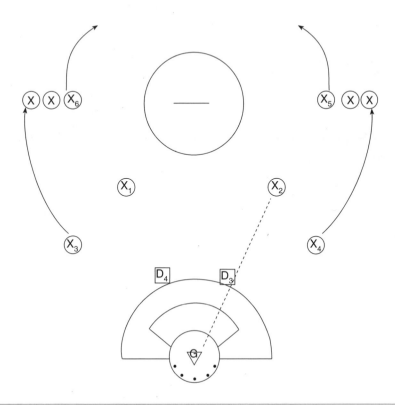

■ **Figure 8.13b** Four-on-Two Continuous Drill *(continued)*.

Name.   Five-on-Five Half-Field (I/A)

Purpose.   To teach the attack to look for fast-break opportunities but then to be patient and to possess the ball until a scoring opportunity arises; to teach defense to focus on one-on-one coverage and to support the ball out of the defensive end of the field

Organization.   You need at least 60 yards of space and one goal area with markings to play this game. Use two teams of five players each, plus a goalkeeper if available. Give the ball to the attacking team at one side of the field, 50 yards from the goal. When the attack team hears the starting whistle, it tries to pass or run the ball toward goal. Defense tries to intercept or to create a turnover to gain possession of the ball.

Coaching Points.   Use conditions for the offense (each one met earns the team a point):

- Five passes among the offense before a shot.
- Ball gets behind the goal safely in possession.
- Must use 20 seconds off the clock before a shot.

Use conditions for the defense (each one met earns the team a point):

- Successfully create a turnover against the attack.
- Complete a block or interception.
- Create a successful double-team.
- Everyone touches ball on the goalkeeper clear.
- Successfully clear the ball out of the defensive end and into the center circle.

You can use one or more conditions at a time. Such conditions teach players strategies while still maintaining the essence of the game, which is to score goals. To make this more gamelike, you could give the attack five possessions in which to score and earn conditioned points, while the defense has five opportunities to get a turnover and earn points working the ball out of the defensive end of the field.

Unit 9

What Is Boys' Lacrosse All About?

Chances are, you've experienced the excitement of a lacrosse game. Imagine yourself cradling down the field toward your opponent's goal. You sprint, cradling the ball, aware of opponents closing in on you. You look for a teammate to pass to. Suddenly, a defender moves to you, and your teammate is open. You pass to him, and he unleashes a shot toward the goal and scores. You feel the exhilaration of the speed and teamwork of lacrosse.

It's time to share your love of lacrosse with your team. The first part of this book gave you a good, general understanding of what it takes to coach. Now it's time to develop your comprehension of lacrosse. The next four units of *Coaching Youth Lacrosse* provide you with the basic skills, techniques, tactics, and drills you should teach. (See page 57 in unit 6 for the key to field diagrams.)

Advantages of Lacrosse

The fast-paced game of boys' lacrosse provides players with a high-intensity team sport combining stick skills, speed, endurance, physical contact, and teamwork. Lacrosse combines the team play of basketball, the speed and checking of hockey, and the endurance of soccer.

Lacrosse provides opportunities for success to a variety of athletes—the small quick dodger, the playmaker, the physical player, and the ground-ball man. There is no stereotypical player in lacrosse. Each player makes his own unique contribution to the team in terms of body size, athletic skills, and lacrosse skills. Excellent lacrosse players come in all shapes and sizes.

How Is the Game Played?

Ten players comprise a lacrosse team: three attackers, three midfielders, three defenders, and a goalkeeper. The transitional component of lacrosse provides each player with the opportunity to initiate and participate in both the offensive and defensive parts of the game. Lacrosse shares the principle objectives of soccer and hockey: that is, to pass or run the ball into the offense area and shoot it past the opponent's goal line.

The rules of the game require each team to keep three players on their opponents' side of the field when the ball is on their own side. Four players (usually the three defenders and the goalie) are required to stay in their end when their offense has possession of the ball. This rule provides a six-player versus six-player situation (really six offense against seven defense when the goalie is counted) that results in the "even" play of the game. Six offensive players pass, dodge, cut, and shoot as six defensive players, with their goalie, protect their goal.

The three attackers designated primarily as offensive players combine with the three midfielders to play settled offense (six-on-six) when they possess the ball on their opponents' half of the field. The midfielders are truly transitional players who play on both ends of the field, offense and defense. The three midfielders combine with three defenders and the goalie to defend their goal when the ball is in their end.

The six-on-six aspect is only one component of the game, and the transitional component provides many fast-break and unsettled situations where the offense may outnumber the defense by a six-to-five, five-to-four, or four-to-three margin. These unsettled situations arise frequently throughout the game and provide many exciting scoring opportunities.

Boys' Versus Girls' Lacrosse

Many differences and similarities exist between boys' and girls' lacrosse. The objective of both is the same. The players (12 on a girls' team and 10 on a boys' team), through passing, scooping, dodging, and team tactics, try to shoot the ball into their opponents' six-foot by six-foot goal area. Both the boys' and girls' versions of the game provide fast, action-packed opportunity for team play and scoring.

The differences in required protective equipment and stick and field regulations, however, give each version a distinctly unique quality. Boys use longer sticks than girls do, and the pockets in their sticks are deeper. Boys must wear helmets, gloves, and arm and shoulder pads because boys' rules, unlike girls', permit body checking. Because boys' lacrosse players are allowed more body contact, their rules are specifically designed to minimize injuries, and the continual advances in protective equipment provide an added safety factor.

Age Guidelines

Young people approximately age six and older can play lacrosse. Young players can develop the basic skills of throwing, catching, scooping, defending, and dodging that allow them to enjoy the game of lacrosse. Young players may enjoy a modified version of field lacrosse with a reduced field, fewer players, and no offside rules.

A popular version of youth field lacrosse is called *pinball lacrosse*, which uses a reduced number of players and a goalie against an equal number of opponents on a small field (seven versus seven on a 30-by-60-yard field, for example) and permits all players to move freely from the offensive end to the defensive end without the offside regulations. These modifications combine the flow of a basketball game with the action and checking of traditional lacrosse. Reducing the number of players and allowing them to move freely between the offensive and defensive ends of the field gives young players the opportunity to handle the ball more often and to participate in both the offensive and defensive tactics of the game.

Ball and Field Dimensions

Boys' lacrosse is played on a field similar in size to soccer and football fields. An official lacrosse field is 110 yards long and 53-1/2 to 60 yards wide.

The field is marked with a center line, which is used during the face-off and when play is resumed after an offside penalty. On both sides of the center line there is an area designated as a restraining box. The goal cages are surrounded by an 18-foot-diameter crease circle (see figure 9.1).

The solid rubber ball is between seven and three-quarters and eight inches around and weighs between five and five and one-quarter ounces. The ball is usually completely white, but a yellow or orange ball may be used for improved visibility.

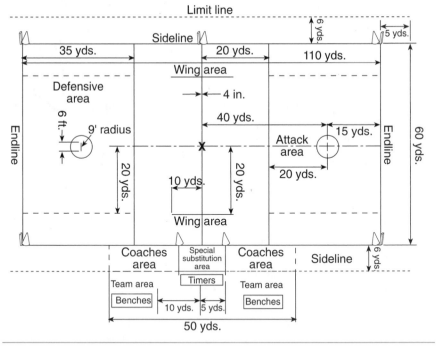

■ **Figure 9.1**　The lacrosse field of play.

Player Equipment

All boys' lacrosse players must wear a protective helmet, padded gloves, arm pads, shoulder pads, a mouthpiece, an athletic supporter, and a protective cup (see figure 9.2). Some players also wear rib pads for additional protection. Require players to wear *all* protective equipment during all practices and games.

Keep two factors in mind when selecting sticks for the beginning player: stick length and pocket type. Young players should begin with a stick with a shaft as long as their arm, or between 30 and 40 inches (see figure 9.3). Beginning players and coaches should not be restricted by the minimum length rule of 40 inches required in the boys' high school and college game. Instead, take into consideration the size of the participant and select a stick length that is comfortable for each player. Move players toward a 40-inch stick as they get older and bigger. When defenders have developed good fundamentals, they can increase the length of the stick to 48 to 60 inches. The soft mesh pocket is a good choice for beginning players at each position. It makes catching and throwing easier and helps with overall skill development. The traditional strung pocket is more difficult to break in and initially makes catching more difficult, but it also results in a stiffer pocket that requires more maintenance.

Players may not alter their sticks to gain an unfair advantage against their opponents. The pockets on boys' sticks can be deeper than in the girls' game, but too deep a pocket often results in the ball catching on the strings and hooking down toward the ground during a pass. It is also illegal—and results in up to a three-minute nonreleasable penalty (depending on regional rules)—for a pocket to be so deep that the top of the ball is visible below the bottom edge of the sidewall when a player holds the stick parallel to the ground at eye level. This rule does not apply to the goalie's stick. In a nonreleasable penalty, a player must serve the full penalty, even if the man-up team scores a goal.

Player Positions

Each of the four basic positions in boys' lacrosse has primary responsibilities, but a successful lacrosse team is one in which all players work together and blend positional duties with team play.

Attack

The three attackers are traditionally the primary ball handlers, passers, scorers, and feeders. They are finesse players who play directly in front of and behind the goal. Attack players need to have excellent stick skills and accuracy.

Midfield

The three midfielders are the all-purpose players. They must have great speed and stamina because they play on both the offensive and defensive ends of the field. The midfielders are involved in a lot of transitional play, and teams often have two to three groups of midfielders. Midfielders are a team's workhorses.

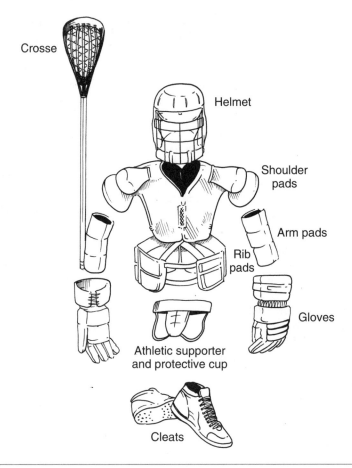

■ **Figure 9.2** Equipment for boys' lacrosse.

Defense

The defenders match up defensively on the opposition's attackers. They are involved in the clearing game (getting the ball out of their defensive half) and often begin the transition from defense to offense after receiving an outlet pass from the goalie or scooping a ground ball. Defense players need excellent stick skills and good agility.

Goalie

The goalie is the last line of defense and also the leader in the defensive unit. He is responsible for stopping the ball from entering the goal and for initiating the transition to offense by outletting (passing) the ball to a teammate. Goalies need to be fearless and to have above-average stick skills.

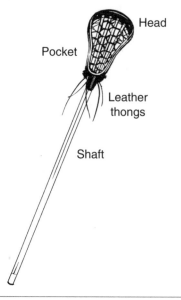

Head

Pocket

Leather thongs

Shaft

■ **Figure 9.3** Parts of a stick.

Offensive Formations

The positioning of the six offensive players who have the ball on their opponent's end of the field depends on the skills and experience of the players and on your personal preferences. Place players where they can use their athletic and lacrosse skills best.

Offensive team formations are described this way:

1. By the number of players positioned in the midfield (positioned at the top of the restraining box). These players are usually midfielders.
2. By the number of players positioned on the crease (directly in front of the goal mouth) and extending out to the wing area. These players can be attackers or midfielders.
3. By the number of players positioned behind the goal. The players in these positions are usually attackers.

A few traditional formations include the 3-1-2, the 2-2-2 , the 2-3-1 , and 1-4-1 (see figure 9.4, a-d).

Teams play two kinds of defense in lacrosse: man-to-man and zone. Man-to-man defense in lacrosse is very similar to man-to-man defense in basketball. Each player guards one assigned opponent, and all other teammates help out if the ball carrier beats his defender. Man-to-man defense concepts give beginning players the tactical knowledge they need to understand the game better.

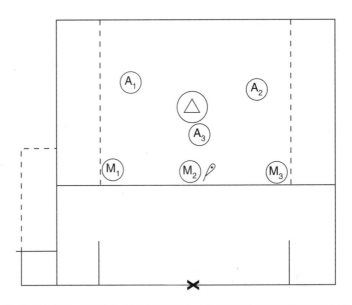

■ **Figure 9.4a** Power lacrosse from the 3-1-2 alignment.

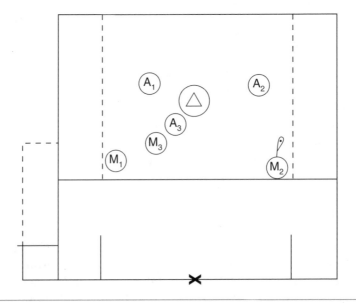

■ **Figure 9.4b** Power lacrosse from the 2-2-2.

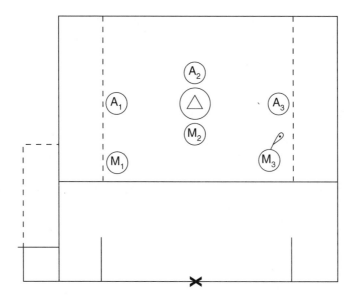

■ **Figure 9.4c**   Power lacrosse from the 2-3-1.

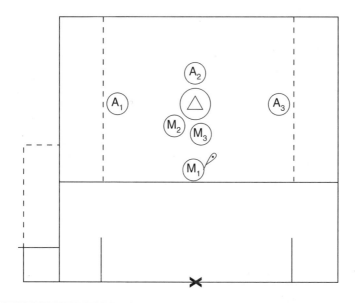

■ **Figure 9.4d**   Power lacrosse from the 1-4-1.

In zone defense, players defend specific areas and the players who enter them. Zone defense can be effective, but young players should learn man-to-man skills and tactics first and then assimilate them later into zone defense strategies.

Officials

One or two individuals with knowledge of lacrosse rules officiate each game. Officials enforce the rules to ensure a safe, fair, and fun contest. Officials also require good behavior from players and coaches. You can be a big help to officials by behaving appropriately and emphasizing disciplined play. The illustrations in appendix D show the signals lacrosse officials use during a game. Get familiar with these signals and teach them to your players.

Length of Game

A lacrosse game consists of four quarters with short breaks after the first and third quarters and a 10- to 15-minute halftime break between the 2nd and 3rd quarters. Adjust the length of a quarter between six and twelve minutes according to the age and experience of the participants. Use a 15-minute running clock per half for players 6 to 8 years old and a 20-minute running clock per half for 9- and 10-year-olds. Use an 8- to 10-minute start/stop clock for 13- to 15-year-olds. (A running clock never stops. A start/stop clock starts and stops as it would in a regulation game.)

Starting and Restarting the Game

At the beginning of each quarter and after each goal, a player from each team faces off. The two face-off players crouch at the center of the field facing their opponent's half of the field. Their sticks are one inch apart on the ground and parallel to the midline (see figure 9.5). The referee places the ball between the heads of their sticks, steps away, and blows the whistle. The two face-off players and their remaining midfield teammates attempt to gain possession of the ball. The attack and defensive players must stay in their respective restraining boxes until the referee signals that one team has gained possession.

If team A passes or carries the ball across the sideline or endline, the referee awards the ball to team B, with one exception. When the ball goes out of bounds on a shot to goal, the referee awards the ball to the team whose player is closest to it. A shot on goal gives either team an opportunity to gain possession of the ball after a shot. Remember: The referee awards the ball to the player closest to the spot where the ball goes out of bounds, which means offensive players should back up shots. Defenders and goalies also have the opportunity to gain possession of the ball.

■ **Figure 9.5**   Face-off.

When the ball goes out of bounds on the sideline or endline, a coach can request that the scorer sound the horn for the purpose of substitution. The official's whistle stops the clock, and either team can substitute at this point. The clock also stops on any personal or technical foul.

Substitutions

Substitution in lacrosse can take place at any point in the game if they are done "on the fly," as in hockey. Players (usually midfielders) can run off the field through the designated substitution area (see figure 9.1 on page 136). As one player exits the field, another steps on. With youth players, however, you should try to substitute players in a settled situation so they can see their position on the field.

Be aware of the offside rule in all substitutions on the fly that involve attackers or defenders. Have players exit and enter on their respective defensive or offensive sides of the midline. For example, if a defender is subbing on the fly, he should exit the field on the defensive end, and the player entering should enter the game on the defensive end after his teammate has exited.

Rules

Lacrosse rules allow safe, continuous, free-flowing games. Even though lacrosse rules allow body and stick checking, limitations provide for a physical but safe game. Different leagues have different body-checking rules for each age group, ranging from no body checking to limited body checking.

A player may body check any opponent within five yards of a loose ball, including the ball carrier, by contacting him from the front or side above the knees and below the shoulders.

Stick checking is legal; however, a player must direct his check at his opponent's stick in an attempt to dislodge the ball. The ball carrier's glove is considered part of the stick and can be checked (although pounding on the gloves is illegal), but stick checks are not allowed to any other part of an opposing player. Infractions result in a one-minute slashing penalty.

Personal Fouls

Lacrosse categorizes two varieties of fouls: personal fouls and technical fouls. Personal fouls are the more serious of the two and often result in the offending player serving a one-minute penalty in a sideline area designated as the penalty box. In severe cases, personal fouls can result in two- or three-minute penalties or in expulsion from the game. These rare situations usually result from excessive slashing, fighting, or other poor behavior. Here are the specific personal fouls called in a game:

cross checking—Using the portion of the stick handle that is between the hands to check or push an opponent.

illegal body checking—Hitting an opponent from the rear, at or below the knees, or above the shoulders or hitting an opponent when he does not possess the ball or is not within five yards of the ball.

slashing—Striking an opponent anywhere except on his stick or on the gloved hand holding the stick.

tripping—Obstructing an opponent at or below the knees with the stick, hands, arms, feet, or legs.

unsportsmanlike behavior—Any conduct an official considers unsportsmanlike. No profanity, on the field or on the bench, is permitted in youth lacrosse.

Technical Fouls

Penalties for technical fouls are less severe than personal fouls and they depend on which team has possession of the ball when the penalty occurs. If the team who commits the technical foul has the ball or if neither team has possession of the ball, the fouled team gets the ball and the fouling team serves no penalty time. If the fouled team has possession of the ball at the time of the technical foul, the official administers a 30-second penalty to the offending player or team.

Other Infractions

These other infractions can be called during a game:

crease violation—Contact with the goalkeeper or his crosse while the goalkeeper and the ball are within the goal crease area, whether or not the goalkeeper has the ball in his possession. Any interference with the goalie results in the official indicating a "play on" situation or awarding the ball to the goalkeeper's team at the center of the field.

holding—Impeding the movement of an opponent by holding him with the head of the crosse or by using a portion of the stick handle.

interference—A player's impeding, in any manner, the free movement of an opponent, except in these circumstances: that opponent has possession of the ball, the ball is in flight and is within five yards of the player, or both players are within five yards of the ball.

offside—A team fails to keep three players in the offensive half of the field or four players in the defensive half.

pushing—Pushing an opponent from any direction. "Equal pressure" is allowed. A push is exerting pressure after contact is made; it is not a violent blow.

An attacking player may never go into the opponent's goal crease. Any offensive player who touches the crease circle or lands inside the circle causes his team to lose possession of the ball. If the defense has gained possession when the crease violation occurs, the ball is awarded to the offended team at the center of the field.

Scoring

A goal scores one point when the ball crosses through the imaginary plane formed by the rear edges of the goal line, the goal posts, and the top cross bar. Most goals are shot, but goals also count when a player kicks the ball in or when the ball rolls in after hitting an offensive or defensive player.

Boys' Lacrosse Terms to Know

backup—An attackman's move into a position to regain possession after a shot. Also refers to an off-ball defender who positions himself so he can support a teammate guarding the ball carrier.

checking—Attempting to dislodge the ball from the opponent's stick by stick or body contact.

clear—A pass or run to advance the ball from the defensive to the offensive half of the field.

close defense—The three defensive players who play immediately behind and in front of their goal, and who are responsible for covering the three opposing attackers player for player. Close defenders often use a stick with a longer handle than midfielders or attackers use.

cradling—Moving the arms and wrists to keep the ball in the stick pocket and ready for passing or shooting.

crease—The circle, with a nine-foot radius, around each goal.

cut—Movement of an offensive player without the ball to free himself to receive a pass or shot.

dodge—The ball carrier's move to elude an opponent.

extra-man offense (EMO)—The offensive unit's numerical advantage that results from at least one member of the opposite team serving time in the penalty box.

fast break—An offensive transition play resulting from a numerical advantage over the defense, traditionally a 4-on-3 advantage.

feed—A pass to a teammate in scoring position.

goal line extended (GLE)—An imaginary line that runs parallel to the endline from the goal posts to the sideline.

ground ball—A loose ball.

hold—A legal technique used by defensive team members to push their opponent away from the goal. A defender can apply legal holds with his hands, arms, and body to the side or front of the attacker.

holding—Illegally impeding an opponent from moving forward or dodging. A holding violation usually occurs when a defender impedes the progress of the ball carrier with his stick.

hole—The area immediately outside of the crease in front of the goal.

invert—To carry the ball in front of the goal (for an attacker) or behind the goal (for a midfielder) to isolate the ball carrier.

isolation (iso)—The space created for the ball carrier to dodge an opponent in a one-on-one situation. The ball carrier and the teammates work together to create the space.

man-ball—Tactic of one man's scooping a loose ball while a teammate body checks the opponent closest to the ball but within the legal five-yard distance.

man-down defense (MDD)—The defensive unit that is outnumbered by at least one player as the result of one or more of its players serving time in the penalty box.

on the fly—How substitutions are made while the clock is running. One player runs off the field through the legal substitution area and another runs on after the first player is completely off the field.

pick—An offensive tactic in which an off-ball player stands motionless to block the path of a player defending the ball carrier or a cutter.

pinch—Position of off-ball defenders who move into the hole to support the defender covering the ball carrier.

riding—Preventing the defenders from advancing the ball from their defensive end of the field to their own offensive end of the field.

scoop—Technique of picking up a loose ground ball.

screen—An offensive tactic in which a player stands in front of the goalie to obscure his vision when another offensive teammate is dodging to shoot from the midfield area.

slide—A move by an off-ball defender off his assigned attacker to block a ball carrier moving unobstructed to the goal.

square-up—Body-on-body, stick-on-stick defensive position.

unsettled situation—A situation in which the defense has not had an opportunity to set up.

ward off—The illegal movement of the ball carrier's free arm to deflect the stick check of his opponent.

X—The area directly behind the goal.

Unit 10

What Boys' Lacrosse Skills and Drills Should I Teach?

In unit 4 you learned how to teach lacrosse skills using the IDEA method for practices. Now it's time to consider exactly what lacrosse skills to emphasize and what drills and activities will help your players develop those skills. This section identifies the basic lacrosse skills to teach your players. Expose your players to all the skills so they become well rounded.

Using Lacrosse Drills Effectively

Before we move to the discussion of offensive and defensive lacrosse skills, let us say a word about how to use drills effectively in your practices. The methods of organizing drills for lacrosse depend on the skill level and experience of the players.

Introduce beginner players to skill practice with partner drills. These drills use pairs of players with one ball for each pair. Players stand facing each other about 10 yards apart as they execute single skills with little movement. As players develop skill and confidence, they can practice skills while moving. Remind players to wear all equipment during every aspect of practice, including during drills.

Organize your group drills so that players move and execute basic fundamentals or combinations of fundamentals, such as scooping and passing. The final progression to facilitate skill development involves adding opposition and competition. At this stage, moving players must execute a variety of skills

---

DRILL TYPES

Partner Drills: Players work in pairs; each pair has one ball. Players stand facing each other 8 to 10 yards apart. You can introduce all basic skills with partner drills. The format allows each player to practice the skill with consistent repetition.

Movement Drills: As players become proficient with a skill, organize them into small groups of six to eight players. Give each group a ball and instruct them to practice the skill while moving. Line drills and box drills are good ways to organize movement drills.

Competitive Drills: Using drills that include movement with opposition is a challenging way to enhance skill development. Small-group activities that have a competitive component provide game-like situations to improve skill and tactical knowledge. Grid drills, unsettled situations, and half-field drills provide an opportunity to practice skills under pressure.

with resistance from opposing players. A balanced combination of drills that includes partner, movement, and competitive work provides a variety of learning experiences and helps keep the players' attention. Make skill development fun for players. Keep instruction concise, and change drills frequently to keep players focused. To help you select which drills match the skill level of your players, we've labeled every drill with either a *B* for beginner, *I* for intermediate, or *A* for advanced.

GENERAL LACROSSE SKILLS

Ready Position

Develop the basic ready position for catching and throwing by having a player hold the stick with his arms at his side and the stick parallel to the ground. His hands are hip width apart, the palm of his top hand faces forward, and his bottom hand covers the butt of the stick with that palm facing his body (figure 10.1). The player then raises the head of his stick to the off-ear position on the same side as his dominant hand.

Cradling

Cradling is often the first skill that the beginning player learns. By coordinated and rhythmic motion of the arms and hands, the player positions the ball in the center of the pocket and develops a "feel" for the ball (figure 10.2).

Bottom-Handed Upright Cradle

The bottom-handed upright cradle allows the player to carry the ball in the ready position where he can pass, shoot, and dodge. In this cradle, the bottom hand cradles the stick and the stationary top hand is the guide hand. The bottom-handed cradle is best used in open space where the ball carrier is not under immediate pressure from a defender.

Teach players to follow these steps for the bottom-handed upright cradle:

1. Initiate the cradling motion by holding the stick diagonally across the body with the head of the stick in the ready position.
2. Bend the top arm to form a 90-degree angle at the elbow. The thumb and index finger encircle the shaft of the stick.
3. Use the bottom hand to cradle the stick: Begin with the palm facing the body and rhythmically rotate the bottom wrist out and in.

■ **Figure 10.1**   The ready position.

■ **Figure 10.2**   Cradling.

Top-Handed Cradle

The top-handed cradle is best in situations where the ball carrier is pressured by a defender and needs to shield the ball and his stick. The top hand initiates the cradling motion and the stationary bottom hand is the guide hand.

Teach your players to perform the top-handed cradle this way:

1. Begin in the ready position with the stick diagonally across your body (figure 10.3a).
2. Begin the cradle with the palm of the top hand facing the body. Rotate your wrist out and back rhythmically (figure 10.3b).
3. Feel the ball in the center of your pocket (figure 10.3c).

Throwing

Many of the principles of throwing the ball in lacrosse are similar to those in baseball. Teach new players the throwing motion by demonstrating a one-handed throw.

To throw correctly, the player must develop these skills:

1. Hold the stick in the ready position with the head of the stick to the side and above the ear (figure 10.4a).

■ **Figure 10.3** Top-handed cradle.

2. Turn so that your shoulders are perpendicular to the target, pointing the off-stick shoulder at the target (figure 10.4a).

3. To initiate the throwing motion, throw with the top hand, pull with the bottom hand, and step with the front foot toward the target (figure 10.4b).

4. Throw the ball to the receiver's stick side and to the head of his stick as he holds it in the ready position.

5. Follow through and carry the stick to a position with the head pointing at the target and the stick parallel to the ground (figure 10.4c).

■ **Figure 10.4**   Throwing.

Error Detection and Correction for Throwing

The most effective method for moving the ball in lacrosse is by passing. Passing accuracy is paramount in becoming an accomplished player.

ERROR: Lack of accuracy

CORRECTION

Follow the steps in performing a correct throw.

Catching

Players must know how to catch the ball consistently while running or standing still. Catching involves proper stick positioning, hand-eye coordination, and a soft touch.

Catching on the Stick Side

Teach players to catch on the stick side first. The receiver pulls the head of the stick back slightly to decelerate the ball as it reaches the pocket.

To catch on the stick side, players should follow these instructions:

1. Be in the ready position to catch a ball coming toward the head of the stick (figure 10.5a).
2. Focus on the ball and watch it enter the pocket (figure 10.5b).
3. Cushion the ball into the pocket by gently relaxing the top hand of the stick as the ball arrives (figure 10.5c).
4. Keep the ball slightly in front of the body.

a   b   c

■ **Figure 10.5** Catching.

Catching on the Off-Stick Side

To catch the ball on the off-stick side, the receiver pushes the stick across his face, similar to the motion of a car's windshield wiper.

Teach players to follow these steps to catch on the off-stick side:

1. Watch the ball into the pocket of the stick and cushion the ball into the pocket.
2. Catch the ball with the pocket facing the passer and bring the stick back across the face to the ready position.

3. Continue to rotate the stick back to the ready position so the stick, pocket, and ball are in position to pass.

Catching Over the Shoulder

A lacrosse player catching the ball while moving away from the passer is similar to a football receiver breaking upfield to receive a pass from his quarterback.

To catch over the shoulder, players must develop these skills:

1. Look back over the shoulder that's on the same side as the head of the stick. (Look over the right shoulder to receive a pass on your right side; turn the head and body to the left to receive a pass on your left side.)

2. "Look" the ball into the pocket of the stick and keep the top hand and the elbow away from your body (figure 10.6, a-b).

a   b

■ **Figure 10.6**   The over-the-shoulder catch.

Error Detection and Correction for Catching

A soft mesh pocket helps beginning players develop catching skills. Proper technique includes decelerating the ball (cushioning it) and catching the ball in the ready position.

ERROR: Reaching out in front of the body to catch the ball

CORRECTION

1. As the ball approaches, begin to move the head of the stick back and in the direction the pass is traveling.
2. Cushion the ball into the pocket.
3. Watch the ball from the passer into the pocket of the stick.
4. Practice catching with the back side of the pocket. Because there is little or no pocket on this side, you must cushion the ball.

Throwing and Catching Drills

Name. Partner Passing—Strong Hand (B)

Purpose. To develop throwing and catching skills with the dominant hand

Organization. Players line up in pairs 10 yards apart and pass the ball back and forth, concentrating on these basic throwing and catching mechanics: Stand perpendicular to receiver, point stick shoulder at receiver, hold stick above head, position hands away from the body, step and throw, and follow through. Players cushion the ball into the stick when receiving it.

Coaching Points. Emphasize the overhand throwing motion and cushioning the ball when catching.

Variations. Catch with the nondominant hand or catch with the dominant hand and switch hands to throw with the nondominant hand.

Name. Right-on-Right Passing and Catching (B)

Purpose. To develop passing and catching skills while moving

Organization. Two lines of three to four players each stand 20 yards apart facing each other. Start the drill with all players holding their sticks in the right hand. The first player in line 1 carries a ball a few steps and throws it with his right hand to the first player in line 2, who is moving toward him. The players follow the pass, then go to the ends of the lines they passed to.

Coaching Points. The receiver and passer must move toward each other, and the receiver should call "Help." The passer should throw the ball overhand and to the ready position of the receiver. Be sure players hold their sticks to the inside and in the ready position when passing and receiving.

Variation.

Left-on-Left: All players throw and catch with the left hand.

Name. Four Corner Passing (I)

Purpose. To practice throwing and catching on the run

Organization. Lines of three or four players stand in each corner of the attack box. The first player in line 1 (the ball carrier) runs toward the first player in line 2 (a receiver). When the ball carrier is midway between line 1 and line 2, he yells "Break," and the receiver breaks toward line 3. The ball carrier passes to the receiver and goes to the end of line 2. When the receiver in line 2 catches the ball and is midway between lines 2 and 3, he yells "Break" and the first person in line 3 becomes the receiver. This process continues around the square until each person has passed and caught the ball two or three times.

Coaching Points. Make sure all play is right-handed, with sticks to the outside. Don't let the receiver break until the ball carrier is in position to make a pass and yells for the break. Instruct the receiver to call "Help" and to give the passer a target in front so he can make a lead pass.

Variation. (1) For advanced practice, have players catch the ball over the shoulder (sticks to the inside) and then change hands to pass the ball (sticks to the outside). (2) The receiver can move directly toward the ball carrier to receive the pass then circle away to pass to the next receiver, who is breaking toward him. The receiver must "move through" the pass and circle away, keeping his stick to the outside. This variation provides excellent practice of clearing skills.

Name. Diamond Passing (A)

Purpose. To practice advanced offensive stick handling

Organization. Four lines of players stand in a diamond formation, each line 12 yards from a marker in the center of the diamond (see figure 10.7). Player 1 (X_1) has the ball and passes it, right-handed, to player 2 (X_2), who has executed a *V* cut by moving in toward the marker and then breaking to the outside. Player 2 (X_2) plays left-handed with his stick to the outside. When player 2 (X_2) catches the ball, his stick changes hands and he passes to player 3 (X_3) with his right hand. Each player follows his pass and goes to the end of that line.

Coaching Points. This drill simulates offensive players on the offensive perimeter who are *V* cutting away from a defender to receive the ball. The cone in the center simulates a defender. Two players move toward each other, and the passer passes the ball to the outside. The offensive player who is two passes away from the ball should anticipate the ball movement and work on timing the *V* cut.

Variation. Add four defenders to introduce pressure. The defenders move out to cover each receiver. When a defender moves out to play the receiver, he should arrive as the ball reaches the receiver and be positioned in the defensive ready position as the ball reaches the receiver: stick down and parallel to the ground, knees bent, and partially sitting. Each off-ball defender moves to the center and keeps his head moving to watch both his man and the ball.

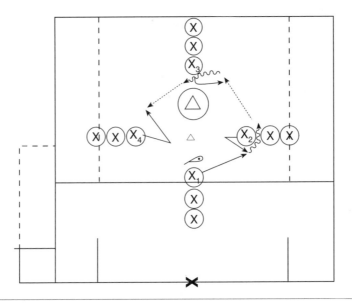

■ **Figure 10.7** Diamond Passing Drill.

Name. Over-the-Shoulder Throwing and Catching (A)

Purpose. To practice throwing and catching over the shoulder

Organization. Two lines of three or four players stand 20 yards apart facing each other. Player 2 in line 1 begins with the ball and moves to his right. When he yells "Break," player 1 in his line breaks with his stick in the right-handed, over-the-shoulder position. As player 1 receives the ball, he looks to line 2. Player 2 in line 2 calls "Help," and receives the pass. Player 2 in line 2 now moves laterally to his right and yells "Break," as player 1 in line 2 breaks with his stick in the right-handed, over-the-shoulder position. After passing, each player goes to the end of the opposite line.

Coaching Points. To receive a pass, players should keep the stick at helmet level. The receiver should look over his shoulder on the side he will catch the ball and follow the ball with his eyes into the pocket of the stick.

MAN, BALL, RELEASE, HELP

Verbal communication enables teammates to work together to win ground balls. These words cue teammates.

"Man": A teammate within five yards of a loose ball may choose to body check or shield an opponent from a loose ball. He calls "Man" and clears the way for a teammate to scoop the ball. He may make body contact only from the front or side and within five yards of the ball.

"Ball": The player going for the loose ball calls "Ball" to alert his teammates that he has an opportunity to scoop the ball.

"Release": After a player has scooped the ball, he yells "Release" to alert teammates that he has the ball. A technical foul of interference results if a player makes body contact with an opponent after a teammate secures possession.

"Help": Players off the ball move to receive a pass from the scooper. An open player alerts the scooper of his position by calling "Help."

Scooping

The ability for individual players to scoop up loose balls contributes to the success of team play. The team that can "swarm" the ground ball and gain possession controls the tempo of the game.

To scoop properly, players should follow these instructions:

1. Move the stick out to the side and almost parallel to the ground (figure 10.8a).
2. Bend at the knees and at the waist as you approach the ball (figure 10.8a).
3. Lower the head of the stick and the butt hand, and accelerate through the ball (figure 10.8b).
4. Hit the ground approximately six inches in front of the ball with the stick. The scooping motion should carry the stick several inches in front of the ball.
5. Concentrate totally on the ball with your head down.
6. Plant the left foot to the side and close to the ball when scooping.
7. Bring the head of the stick to the ready position and continue to run to an open area (figure 10.8c).
8. Look up the field and be ready to pass or dodge (figure 10.8d).

The scooper moves through the ball and continues to move away from pressure by keeping his body between the defender and the ball.

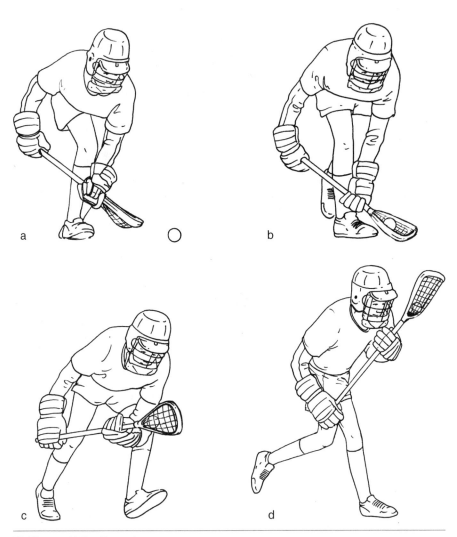

■ **Figure 10.8** Scooping.

Scooping Drills

Name. One-on-One Scooping With Outlet (B/I)

Purpose. To develop scooping and passing skills under pressure

Organization. Three lines of players stand five yards apart. One line is the outlet "help" line and the other two lines compete for possession of the loose ball. The coach stands in between the two lines and rolls out a ground ball. The player that scoops the ball passes to the outlet, while the opponent plays defense. Each player goes to the end of his line.

Coaching Points.   Instruct players to scoop through the ball and to run away from pressure. They should protect their stick after scooping the ball by keeping the body between the defender and the stick. This is a good situation in which to execute the "fishhook" by circling away from the defender with the stick shielded. Instruct the outlet player to call "Help" and to move to create a passing lane.

Error Detection and Correction for Scooping

Team success depends on the individual players' scooping skills.

ERROR: Missed scoops

CORRECTION

1. Approach the ground ball at full speed and get low by bending at the knees and the waist.
2. Keep the stick out to the side with the back hand lowered to a position between the knees and hips.
3. Put the head of the stick down six inches in front of the ball.
4. Bring the head of the stick and ball up to the ready position as you complete the scoop.
5. Be ready to pass the ball to an open teammate.

Name.   Partner Scooping and Cradling (B)

Purpose.   To develop scooping skills

Organization.   Players line up in pairs facing each other 10 yards apart. One player has the ball at his feet, and on your command he scoops the ball up and passes it to his partner.

Coaching Points.   Be sure the scooper drops the leg on his off-stick side and bends his knees. His stick goes out to the side and his head goes down to the ball as he scoops through. The back hand must be down to a level between the knees and hip. The scooper must yell "Ball" and "Release," and the receiver yells "Help." After scooping the ball, the ball carrier runs several steps and passes to his partner.

Variation.   Players scoop with the nondominant hand.

Name.   Scooping and Passing (B)

Purpose.   To develop scooping and passing skills

Organization.   Two lines of players stand 20 yards apart. Player 2 in line 1 rolls the ball forward to player 1 in line 1, who runs after it and scoops. The scooper goes through the ball, scoops it, and passes it to player 2 in line 2.

Player 2 in line 2 then rolls the ball forward for player 1 in line 2 to scoop. Player 2 in each line then moves up to become player 1. Each player goes to the end of the line that he passed to.

Coaching Points. Require players to use appropriate communication: "Ball," "Release," "Help." The scooper must accelerate through the ground ball and bring the stick quickly to the ready position. He makes the pass as soon as he has control.

Name. Two-on-One Ground Ball Drill (I)

Purpose. To develop skill and teamwork on ground balls

Organization. Three lines of players stand five yards apart. The coach rolls out a ball between the middle player and either of the end lines. The players in two of the lines are teammates and the players in the third line are their opponents. The players in the teammate lines work together against a single opponent to win the ground ball. The player closest to the ball goes to scoop the ground ball, and the other player goes between the ball and the opponent's body to body check him, from the front or side and above the knees, if that player is within five yards of the ball.

Coaching Points. This drill creates an opportunity for a man/ball call between the two teammates. Have players communicate by calling "Man," "Ball," "Release," and "Help" as the play develops. The single player should be an end line and the ball should be rolled between the two teammates to create a man/ball situation.

Face-Offs

The face-off at the center of the field begins play at each quarter and after a goal. The team that consistently gets possession of the ball on the face-off controls the tempo of the game.

During a face-off, two opponents stand at the center of the field, each facing his offensive goal. The two wing midfielders stand ready on the wing lines with their opponents. The attackers and defensemen must stay in their areas until the official signals that one team has possession of the ball or until a loose ball enters the box area. The official places the ball at the center of the field on the ground and instructs both face-off players to assume the face-off position (all face-offs are taken right-handed).

Teach your players the following steps for facing off:

1. Assume a low, crouched position with the feet shoulder width apart and weight evenly distributed.
2. Place the right hand at the top of the shaft or the stick with the palm facing forward and the left hand shoulder width from the top hand.

Rest both hands on the ground, with the handle of the stick parallel to the midfield line.

3. Keep your stick one inch from the ball on the ground, being sure to match the back of your pocket with your opponent's.

4. Keep both hands and both feet to the left of the throat of the cross (see figure 9.5 on page 143).

Clamp and Step Technique

The clamp and step is a basic face-off technique that enables the face-off man to gain possession of the ball himself or to direct the ball to one of his wing players. When the official sounds the whistle, the face-off man proceeds this way:

1. Stay low and step to the head of the stick. Clamp down over the ball with the top hand and drive into the opponent with the right shoulder. At the same time, pull back with the left hand toward your left knee. Coordinate all movements to occur simultaneously.

2. Try to get your head and upper body over the ball, and pivot your hips into the opponent, positioning your body between the ball and the opponent.

3. Direct the ball out to an area or to a wing player.

Dodging

All players in possession of the ball have the opportunity to advance the ball upfield and toward their opponent's goal by passing, running, and dodging. All players should learn several basic dodges. Players in any position can use the face dodge, roll dodge, and bull dodge.

Face Dodge

When a defender rushes at the ball carrier with his stick up, a face dodge is appropriate. The face dodge requires good setup for an effective execution. A ball carrier sets up a face dodge by placing his stick up in the ready position for a pass or shot (figure 10.9a).

Teach players to follow these steps to execute a face dodge:

1. As the defender tries to check your stick, bring the stick across your body from the ready position on the stick side to the opposite side of your body.

2. As you bring the stick across your body, dip your head and shoulders slightly, then drive forward off your left foot (for right-handed players),

cross your right foot over your left, and keep your eyes looking straight ahead (figure 10.9b).

3. Keep two hands on the stick and continue to move away from the rushing defender.

4. Bring the stick back to the ready position on your stick side.

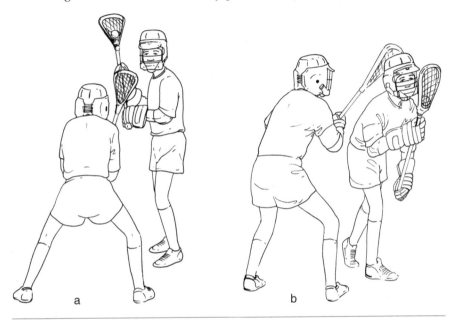

a   b

■ **Figure 10.9** Face dodge.

Roll Dodge

The roll dodge is most effective when a defender overcommits and tries to poke or check the ball carrier's stick.

Players executing a roll dodge must learn the following skills:

1. Plant the foot on the off-stick side with the toe pointing straight ahead (a right-handed player would plant the left foot). Pivot 180 degrees to the off-stick side while bending your knees so that your back is toward the defender (figure 10.10, a-b).

2. Step out with your right foot, plant it, and swing your body around to follow it (figure 10.10c).

3. Continue to run past the defender (figure 10.10d).

■ **Figure 10.10** Roll dodge.

Bull Dodge

Use the bull dodge against a defender who is standing still. The dodger simply fakes to his off-stick side and then runs by, or through, the defender's stick.

Teach players the following bull dodging steps:

1. Roll your shoulders from parallel to the defender's stick to perpendicular to it (figure 10.11a).

2. Move past the defender and use your shoulders and head to protect the stick. The beaten defender may try a desperation stick check (figure 10.11b).

a   b

■ **Figure 10.11** Bull dodge.

Dodging Drill

Name. Line Dodging Drill (B)

Purpose. To develop face, roll, and bull dodging skills

Organization. Two lines of three or four players each stand 20 yards apart face to face. Player 1 in line 1 (the ball carrier) moves forward with a ball as player 1 in line 2 (the defender) moves out to the middle to offer passive defensive resistance. The ball carrier dodges the defender and passes the ball to player 2 in line 2. The former ball carrier then becomes the defender. Instruct the defensive player to set up the offensive dodger in one of three ways: by charging him with his stick low and at the dodger's stick (the dodger roll dodges past the defender), by charging him with his stick up high and at the dodger's stick (the dodger face dodges), or by having the defender stand still (the dodger bull dodges).

Coaching Points. Tell players to keep their sticks tight to their head and body to protect the stick as they move past the defender. The dodger should pass the ball as soon as he is past the defender. Do not allow a dodger to drop the stick back to pass. Work on one dodge at a time, and instruct the defender to make the setup obvious.

Variation. Allow defenders to set up the dodge without your input. Dodgers must react.

OFFENSIVE SKILLS

Midfielders and attackmen must develop skills to maximize offensive opportunities. These skills include ball handling—inside roll, split dodge, one-handed cradling, feeding, shooting, and changing direction—as well as off-ball play—cutting and picking.

Inside Roll

When an attackman drives with the ball from behind the goal, he often finds himself playing directly against a defender on the side of the goal. This area above the goal line extended and at the top of the circle is a good spot for the inside roll. When the ball carrier feels the pressure from the defender on his upfield shoulder, he can perform an inside roll.

To perform an inside roll, a player must follow these steps:

1. Pivot off the front foot (figure 10.12a). For a right-handed player, this is the left foot.
2. Drop the center of gravity by bending at the knees and "sitting down" (figure 10.12b).
3. Keep the stick protected behind the head and body (figure 10.12b).
4. Drop the right foot toward the goal and pivot off the left foot around the defender.
5. Keep the stick parallel to the body and close to the chest during the pivot. Do not switch hands.

After the inside roll, your player will be in great position to shoot on goal (figure 10.12c).

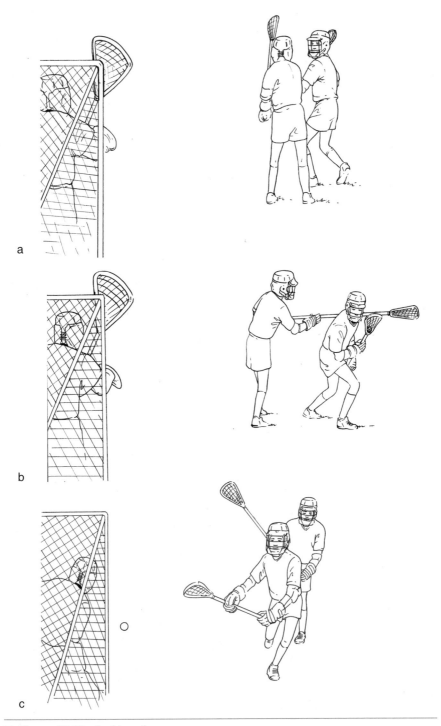

Split Dodge

The ability to handle and shoot the ball with both hands enhances players' effectiveness. All players can use the split dodge to create a shooting opportunity.

Teach players to follow these steps to do a split dodge:

1. Run cradling the ball in the right hand across the field forcing the defender to run parallel and in a hip-to-hip position with the ball carrier (figure 10.13a).
2. Plant the stick-side foot and redirect your body (figure 10.13b), diagonally switching the hands by sliding the left hand to the top of the shaft and placing the right hand at the end of the shaft.
3. Bring the stick quickly across the face (figure 10.13c).
4. Accelerate toward the goal (figure 10.13d).

a

b

c

d

■ **Figure 10.13**   Split dodge.

A young player can start with the ball in his "weak" hand and set up a shot with his preferred (strong) hand by using the split dodge. The right-handed player starts with the ball in the left hand and splits back to the right.

Error Detection and Correction for the Split Dodge

The dodger's ability to bring the stick across his body by switching and sliding the hands allows him to move in either direction. This skill is very similar to a crossover dribble in basketball.

ERROR: Dropping the head of the stick out of the ready area when switching hands

CORRECTION

1. Execute the dodge quickly or else the stick is exposed as you dodge a defender. Make sure that you bring the stick across your body.
2. Plant the stick-side foot (outside foot) and push off this foot toward the inside foot. Then step with the inside foot at a 45-degree angle in the original line of direction.
3. Drive upfield at a 45-degree angle to the defender.
4. Move the stick from hand to hand (ready position to ready position) when dodging. Keep the stick within the frame of the body.

One-Handed Cradle

More advanced offensive players use the one-handed cradling technique to shield and carry the ball when they are under direct pressure from a defensive player.

Teach players to follow these steps to cradle with one hand (figure 10.14):

1. Grasp the stick handle with the top hand about five inches down from the head. Position the thumb of the top hand in front of the handle and pointing up.
2. Position the head of the stick behind your head and shoulders with the shaft perpendicular to the ground.
3. Rotate your shoulders to the side of the body to create a wide body surface for shielding the stick.
4. As you run, use the arm's natural motion to facilitate the cradle. Hold your off-stick hand out from your hip to help protect the stick.

■ **Figure 10.14**
One-handed cradle.

Change of Direction

The ball carrier uses a change of direction to shield the ball from his opponent. This advanced move requires the ball carrier to stop and reverse his direction. The ball carrier concentrates first on protecting his stick; he can work on speed as he becomes more skilled.

To change directions, players should follow these instructions:

1. Drive diagonally across the field, plant the foot opposite the stick, and bend the knees. These steps should be executed when a defender slows down the ball carrier or the ball carrier exhausts field space.

2. Pivot away from the defender, keeping the stick protected by your upper body. Keep your body between the defender and the stick.

3. With your back to the defender and as your shoulders and head start to move away from your original line of direction, pull the stick back with the top hand and switch hands.

4. Keep the stick completely shielded from the defender.

Error Detection and Correction for Change of Direction

Players must be able to protect the ball when changing direction against a defender who is applying heavy defensive pressure.

ERROR: Exposing the ball when executing a change of direction

CORRECTION

1. Keep your head and upper body between the defender and your stick.

2. Switch hands on the stick as your shoulders come around.

3. Keep the stick behind your body so that it is completely shielded from the defender. Don't drag the stick behind you after you come out of the dodge.

4. Accelerate when you've completed the change of direction.

Playing Without the Ball

Even when an offensive player does not have the ball, he must keep moving to make it more difficult for the defense to cover him. The art of playing without the ball requires learning where and when to move.

The V Cut

The *V* cut enables a potential receiver to create a passing lane on the perimeter of the defense. The receiver moves four or five steps in toward the goal, then quickly breaks away toward the passer (figure 10.15, a-c). Timing is important, and both the passer and the receiver move toward each other so the pass is short. Both players have their sticks to the outside of the defender.

Cutting

A cutting opportunity exists whenever an off-ball defender watches the ball carrier instead of the man he is covering. Each off-ball offensive player must watch his teammate with the ball and his own defender to spot a cutting opportunity.

Cutters must learn these skills:

1. Cut to the ball carrier at full speed with your stick in the ready position. The best time to cut is when the defender is ball watching.
2. Call "Help" to get the feeder's attention.
3. Time the cut. Make eye contact with the feeder and cut when he is ready to pass the ball.
4. Discontinue the cut and round back to your original position if you don't receive a pass in front of the goal. Do not crowd the feeder's space by moving into the feeder's area with your defender.
5. Move laterally to get your stick clear of your defender's stick.

Cutting Drill

Name. Playing the Cutter (B)

Purpose. To develop offensive and defensive cutting skills

Organization. Two lines of midfielders, one offensive and one defensive, stand at the top of the attack box. One middie from the defensive line steps forward to defend the cutting offensive middie. Two attackmen, each with a ball, stand behind the goal and a goalie is in position. On your signal, the cutter runs at the defender, fakes, and cuts to an attackman. That attackman feeds him.

Coaching Points. Be sure the cutter head fakes as he moves to the feeder and that he angles to the edge of the crease to avoid running into it. Teach the defender to watch the cutter's hips—not his head, shoulders, or eyes—as the defender shuffles back and cushions the cutter on his approach. Listen for the goalie to call "Check" as the feeder passes the ball into crease

■ **Figure 10.15** *V* cutting.

area, and watch the defensive middie check downward on the offensive midfielder's stick. Tell the feeder to move laterally when feeding.

Variations.   Two attackmen can pass a ball back and forth so the defensive middie must react to a variety of ball locations. The defensive midfielder must continuously watch his man and the ball. ("head on a swivel"). Add an additional attackman and defender to provide practice using a pick and defending the pick and cut.

Picking

Picks are used to free a teammate for a shot or for a cut to the feeder. The ball carrier, pick man, and cutter work together to create a scoring opportunity. The pick man stands motionless to allow his teammate to run his defender into the pick. The pick man must prepare for and protect against contact, because his teammate's defender might run into him.

Shooting

A team can't win if it can't score goals. Shots fall into two categories, each with its own techniques and strategies: inside (within 10 yards of the goal) and outside (from 10 to 18 yards away from the goal). Help your players practice and develop both types.

Inside Shooting

Many inside shots result from a feed behind the goal to the shooter cutting toward the goal from the front. In this situation, the shooter takes one cradle as he catches the ball and then he shoots the ball overhand, low and to the far pipe. For example, if the shooter catches the ball on the right side of the goal (facing the goal from in front of the cage), he cradles it to gain control and then shoots low and toward the left goal post. Imagine a triangle in each of the four corners of the goal, measuring one foot by one foot along the posts. These are called the "scoring triangles," and your players should shoot to these areas. Depending on the goaile's position, players can also shoot for open net.

Teach your players how to change the plane of the ball when they take a shot. Changing the plane refers to catching the ball up high and changing the direction of the ball by shooting low. Most goalies keep their body and stick up high when the ball is close to the goal, which makes them vulnerable to a low shot.

BASIC PRINCIPLES OF SHOOTING

1. Shoot overhand and follow through (figure 10.16, a-c).
2. Always look for the open space in the goal, shooting low and away from the goalie. A common mistake is to look at the goalie, his stick, or the goal pipes.
3. Bounce outside shots.
4. Change the plane of inside shots. For example, catch the ball high and shoot it low.

a   b   c

■ **Figure 10.16**   Shooting.

Outside Shooting

A ball carrier dodging and moving toward the goal or a player who receives a pass and has time to wind up has the opportunity to take an outside shot. Outside shots that bounce in front of the goalie have a better chance of being successful than direct shots do. A prepared shooter tests the ground during the pregame warm-up to study how the ball will bounce. He locates a spot far enough out from the goal mouth to prevent the goalie from catching the ball in the air but close enough to allow the ball to bounce into but not over the goal. Aiming for a spot about one foot in front of the crease circle usually brings success.

Shooting on the Run

When shooting on the run, the player drives diagonally toward the cage.

Teach these skills, which are similar to inside shooting skills, to players learning to shoot on the run:

1. Shoot the ball overhand and follow through to the target. Shoot right-handed when driving right and left-handed when driving left.
2. Shoot the ball low and to the far post to the scoring triangle.
3. Use a screen when shooting bounce shots from the outside. Watch for a teammate to position himself in front of the goalie to obscure his vision while you dodge from the front of the goal. The screener positions himself one foot off the crease circle and directly in front of the goalie. As the shot goes past, he turns to look for any rebounds.

Room and Time Shooting

Sometimes the shooter might have time to wind up and shoot the ball after catching a pass. The basic shooting principles apply:

1. Look for a screen and use his feet as a target.
2. Point the off-stick shoulder and foot toward the target.
3. Step with the front foot, cross over with the back foot, and step again with the front foot—a movement similar to throwing a ball for distance. Get your body into the shot!
4. Keeping the head of the stick up high, shoot the ball toward the unguarded post (probably the outside post), and follow through to the goal.

Shooting Drills

Name. Same-Side Shooting (I)

Purpose. To develop catching and inside shooting skills with both hands

Organization. Two lines of feeders stand behind the cage and two lines of cutters and shooters stand at the top of the restraining box. (One line of feeders and one of cutters stand on each side of the goal, and those two lines drill together.) Each of the feeders has a ball. The first cutter cuts to the side of the crease with his stick to the outside, and the first feeder, also with his stick to the outside, moves laterally and up the field to feed the ball to the cutter, who takes an inside shot. Feeders go to the end of the cutters' line, and cutters go to the end of the feeders' line, but all players stay on their original side of the cage. After players have had sufficient practice on one side of the cage, they switch sides. Keep the drill moving quickly to provide ample repetition at feeding, cutting, and shooting.

Coaching Points. Require the feeders to move laterally and up the field to create a feeding lane. The shooter should catch the ball and shoot it to the scoring triangle at the far post.

Variation. Switch roles so that the players behind the cage are cutters and the players at the top of the restraining box are feeders. The feeders feed the cutters coming up the field for a shot.

Name. Drive From the Center and Shoot (B)

Purpose. To practice shooting accurately while on the run

Organization. One line of players faces the goal at the top and in the center of the attack box. Each player in turn runs left or right and shoots the ball with his stick to the outside. Give each player a ball to keep the drill moving quickly.

Coaching Points. Have players execute a bull or split dodge while shooting the ball on the ground toward the far pipe (scoring triangle). Instruct the players to shoot while running; don't allow them to slow down to wind up.

Error Detection and Correction for Shooting

Players often miss the goal because they use poor technique and they don't follow the basic shooting principles.

ERROR: Missing the goal when shooting

CORRECTION

1. Carry the basic techniques of passing over into shooting.
2. Shoot the ball overhand and on the ground when dodging from the midfield. Bounce the ball in front of a screen.
3. When you are in the restraining box and moving away from the center of the goal, shoot with the stick to the outside of the field.
4. Shoot the ball to the unguarded post and to the scoring triangle.
5. Change the plane of the shot when shooting inside. For example, catch the ball up high and redirect it low and to the unguarded post. Always shoot for the scoring triangle.

DEFENSIVE SKILLS

When a team loses possession of the ball, it becomes the defensive team; therefore, all players must develop basic defensive skills.

Defensive Stance

The basic defensive stance in lacrosse is similar to the ready position of a linebacker in football. The defender stands with his feet apart and establishes a low center of gravity so he can move quickly in any direction.

Teach players the following aspects of defensive positioning (figure 10.17):

1. Keep the feet shoulder-width apart.
2. Bend the knees and lower the center of gravity.
3. Bend forward slightly at the waist. The weight of the head and shoulders stays over the feet.
4. Hold the stick parallel to the ground directly in front of you.

Defensive players stay between the ball carrier and the goal—an aim best accomplished by using good footwork with the proper body position.

■ **Figure 10.17** Defensive stance.

Footwork

To build the foundation for effective defensive play, instruct your players how to correctly move their feet and position their bodies in response to the movement of the ball carrier. Basic defensive footwork consists of shuffle steps and hip-to-hip running.

When the ball carrier moves slowly, the defender shuffles his feet and keeps his shoulders square to the ball carrier. When the ball carrier begins to run faster, the defender turns and runs hip to hip with him (figure 10.18). The defender establishes the hip-to-hip position with a crossover step. He pushes off the foot closest to the ball carrier, brings the back foot across the front of the body, turns the hips, and runs.

When the ball carrier runs at the defender, the defender uses a drop step. He drops the leg closest to the ball carrier and "opens his hips" in that direction. The defender then shuffles or runs hip to hip with the ball carrier, depending on the ball carrier's speed.

■ **Figure 10.18** Defensive positioning while running.

KEYS TO CORRECT FOOTWORK

Adapt to the movement of the ball carrier.

1. If he is moving slowly, shuffle.
2. If he is running, run hip to hip.
3. If he runs directly at you, drop step and open your hips in that direction.

Footwork Drill

Name. Agilities (B)

Purpose. To develop footwork fundamentals

Organization. Four lines of players are positioned side by side facing you, 10 yards apart. The first player steps out and reacts to your stick movement and verbal instructions that include the following:

1. Shuffle right and left.
2. Shuffle right and left, then drop and run.
3. Run hip to hip laterally.
4. Shuffle back at a 45-degree angle.
5. Sprint back at a 45-degree angle.
6. Drop step, open hips, and run straight backward.
7. Run at you and, on signal, break down to the defensive ready position.

After the players go through the whole series of seven commands, or a combination of them, they go to the end of the line.

Coaching Points. Keep movement short and require high intensity. Work on one type of footwork at a time.

Stick Position

Teach beginning players to play "preferred-hand defense." The defensive player keeps the stick in his strong hand and moves the head of the stick to keep it in front of the ball carrier. The defender carries his stick at the height of the number on the ball carrier's jersey.

The defender combines good footwork and stick position to keep the ball carrier at least one stick's length away from him. This space, or cushion, between the ball carrier and the defender makes it easier for the defender to react to the ball carrier's dodges and changes of direction.

Error Detection and Correction for Footwork

Correct footwork is the most important component of playing good defense. Reinforce the importance of footwork as the foundation for playing effective defense.

ERROR: Changing from a shuffle to a hip-to-hip run in the wrong situation

CORRECTION

1. Remind defenders to follow the motion pattern of the ball carrier. When the ball carrier moves slowly, the defender shuffles his feet. When the ball carrier runs, the defender crosses over and runs hip to hip with him.

2. Teach players to create a cushion between them and the ball carrier by shuffling back as the ball carrier approaches. When the ball carrier drives straight at a player, the player drop steps and opens his hips in that direction.

Checking

Stick checks won't be effective unless they're preceded by good footwork that puts the defender in good body position. Emphasize that good defensive play requires correct body position combined with correct stick position. Teach players to make their stick checks short, vigorous, aimed at the opponent's stick, and under control.

Poke Check

The poke check is the most basic and most commonly used check. It effectively disrupts the ball carrier without extending the defender into a vulnerable, off-balance position.

To poke check, players should follow these instructions:

1. Assume the basic defensive stance and stick position.

2. With the back hand, push the stick through the thumb and forefinger of the top hand (figure 10.19a). (This motion is a lot like the motion used to shoot pool.)

3. Keep your body a stick's length away from the ball carrier to create a cushion between you.

4. Aim the poke at the ball carrier's bottom hand when he has two hands on his stick (figure 10.19b); aim across the ball carrier's numbers to the head of the stick when he has one hand on the stick.

5. Do not extend your feet or upper body. If you step in toward the ball carrier, he might be able to dodge you.

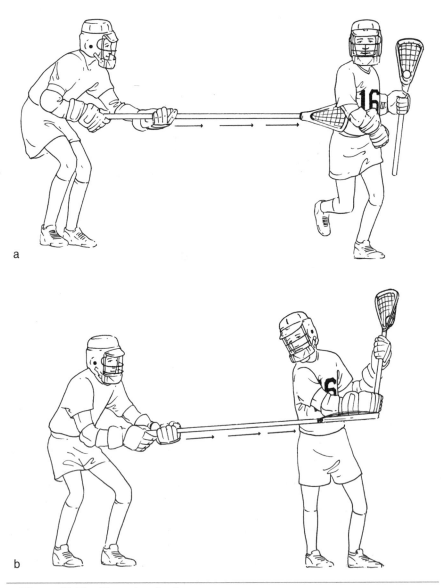

a

b

■ **Figure 10.19** The poke check.

Error Detection and Correction for the Poke Check

Timing and technique are critical to a safe, effective poke check. Make sure your players square up and use good footwork when checking.

ERROR: Lunging and overextending when poke checking

CORRECTION

1. Keep feet parallel when poking. Do not step toward the ball carrier.
2. Keep a cushion between you and the ball carrier.
3. Slide the stick through the top hand.

Slap Check

In the slap check, the defender brings the head of his stick from in front of the ball carrier back into the ball carrier's stick hand and glove.

Players must learn the following skills to slap check:

1. Assume the defensive ready position and hold your stick out in front of the ball carrier at a 45-degree angle (figure 10.20a).
2. Time the delivery of the slap check to coincide with a pass or shot attempt.
3. As the ball carrier places two hands on the stick in preparation for his pass or shot, bring the head of your stick down on his bottom hand (figure 10.20b).

■ Slap Check Drill ■

Name.   Shuffle and Poke or Shuffle and Slap (B/I)

Purpose.   To develop poke check and slap check skills

Organization.   You may conduct this drill without using a ball. Two parallel lines of players stand at the top corner of the attack box. The line closest to the midline is offense, and the line inside the attack box is defense. Signal the first pair of players to step out—the offensive player faces the cage, his stick in his left hand. The defender assumes the defensive ready position with his stick ready to practice the poke check or the slap check. The offensive player jogs across the field as the defender shuffles with him and poke checks or slap checks. Players continue to the opposite top corner and stop. On your signal, the second pair begins. When the entire group has gone in one direction, repeat the drill in the opposite direction.

Coaching Points.   Correct defenders who don't keep shuffling their feet and who lunge toward their opponents.

Variations.   The offensive players can carry a ball to work on stick protection. The ball carrier can alternate between a jog and a run to give the defenders practice in shuffling and running hip to hip.

■ **Figure 10.20**   The slap check.

Body Check

Body checking is part of lacrosse and, when it's combined with good stick skills and sound tactics, it adds another component to team play. Lacrosse is a physical game, but never let physical contact overshadow stick skills and team play.

A player carrying the ball or one within five yards of a loose ball may be legally body checked from the front or side, above the knees and below the shoulders.

A legal body check in lacrosse is most effective in two situations:

- In a loose-ball situation where one defender takes the "ball" and one takes the "man"
- When sliding to a dodger who is closing in on the goal for a shot

A legal body check in lacrosse is similar to a shoulder block in football. A player body checks by running, shoulder down, into an opponent. He makes contact with his shoulder and upper body, never with his head or stick.

Holds

As the ball carrier drives to his goal, the defender must prevent him from moving into a prime shooting area. Proper hold techniques make it possible for the defender to remain in good body and stick position while forcing the ball carrier away from the goal. Defensive players listen for their goalie to yell "Hold." The goalie makes this call when the ball carrier runs into the prime scoring area in front of the goal—the *hole*. The hole area extends 7 yards from the goal posts out to the sideline and 12 yards forward toward the restraining lines.

The goalie calls "Hold" when the ball carrier is slightly outside of these parameters to allow the defender to hear and react to the call. The defender always keeps the head of his stick in front of the ball carrier so he's in position to block a pass or shot.

Forearm Hold

A right-handed defender plays a right-handed ball carrier this way:

1. Hold your right arm with your elbow bent at a 90-degree angle (figure 10.21).
2. Establish a wide base of support. Bend at the knees.
3. Hold the stick at chest level parallel to the ground.

4. Apply pressure to the ball carrier's upfield-shoulder side at a point below the armpit. Keep space between your forearm and chest.

5. Use steady pressure to prevent the ball carrier from moving to the goal. Separate from the ball carrier when he moves out of the hole area.

■ **Figure 10.21** Forearm hold.

Fist Hold

A right-handed defender plays a left-handed ball carrier this way:

1. Extend your hands completely away from your body as you prepare to apply pressure to the ball carrier. Slide your hands together by bringing the top hand down to meet the bottom hand.

2. Establish a wide base of support. Bend at the knees.

3. Hold the stick at waist level, parallel to the ground.

4. Apply pressure to the ball carrier's upfield-shoulder side at the point below the armpit, applying pressure with the fists. Keep your arms fully extended to keep a cushion between you and the ball carrier.

5. Move away from the ball carrier after you've pressured him away from the goal.

Defensive Holding Drill

Name.   Defensive Hold Drill (I)

Purpose.   To develop correct hold techniques

Organization.   Two parallel lines of players stand at the top corner of the penalty box. The line closest to the midline is offense and the line inside the attack box is defense. On your signal, the first pair of players steps out. The offensive player faces the cage with his stick in his left hand, and the defender assumes the defensive ready position. The offensive player jogs across the field and steps up to the attack box every six to eight yards. As the offensive player steps up to the line, the defender steps up to execute the correct hold technique. After the first pair has completed its second step-up and hold, the next pair begins the drill. The pairs continue across the box to the opposite corner. No offensive or defensive player should cross over the attack box line.

Coaching Points.   Check that the defender places his feet and shoulders parallel to the attack box line, drops his center of gravity, and extends his hands during the hold.

Error Detection and Correction for Holds

A defender must always keep his stick in front of the ball carrier in the passing and shooting lane.

ERROR: Incorrect hold technique

CORRECTION

1. When the ball carrier reaches the hole area, assume the defensive ready position: bend your knees, "sit," and keep your feet parallel to each other.
2. Keep your stick in the ball carrier's passing and shooting lane.
3. Keep your hands extended from your body on the forearm and fist holds as you apply pressure to the upfield-shoulder side below the armpit.
4. Do not step forward with the back foot and open up space when executing a hold; doing so invites the ball carrier to roll inside.

Playing the Cutter

When an off-ball offensive player makes a cut to the ball, cover him tightly:

1. Holding your stick up, run hip to hip with the cutter.
2. Check down on the cutter's stick if his teammate feeds him the ball.

Defenders playing the cutter must communicate because a defender may not see the ball. He depends on the goalie to yell "Check" to signal him that a feed is being made to his man. Cutters instinctively raise their eyes and hands as the ball arrives. When a defender sees that move, it is time to check.

Playing the V Cut

When an offensive player breaks away from the goal area to receive a pass on the perimeter, the defender moves out to cover the receiver. As the ball is in the air, the defender moves out and breaks down (bends at the knees and partially sits) at least one stick's length away from the receiver. He keeps his stick parallel to the ground and ready to poke check. He can now move easily in any direction.

Unit 11

How Do I Get My Boys to Play as a Team?

Young athletes must develop individual skills, but no matter how skillful players are as individuals, they must learn team tactics and be able to work together as a unit. The most effective method of teaching team tactics and team play is through small-group competitive drills, which enable players to emphasize one or more team tactics. And small-group drills are fun!

Offensive Team Concepts

You can use several offensive team concepts to create scoring opportunities when the offense does not have a numerical advantage (called the *settled game*):

1. *Develop field sense.* First, offensive players should watch their teammate with the ball and also the teammate's defender. Secondly, when an off-ball defender turns his head or back and removes his attention from the man he is covering, that offensive player has an excellent opportunity to cut to his teammate for a feed or shot. (Viewing videos is very helpful for both coaches and players.)

2. *Stay balanced.* The six offensive players work together to ensure that the field is balanced. Field balance prevents crowding, places players in position to back up shots, and positions players to make the transition to defense should the team lose possession.

3. *Give and go, or "backdoor" cut.* Players pass and then cut to receive a return pass. This tactic creates space for the ball carrier and often sets up a scoring opportunity.

4. *Dodge.* When the ball carrier receives a pass, he looks for an open area, dodges toward it, and goes to the goal for a shot or pass. The ball carrier doesn't dodge unless a teammate has cleared space. If an off-ball defender slides to the ball carrier, the ball carrier passes to an open teammate.

5. *Create space for the dodger.* Players adjacent to the ball carrier cut through and away from the ball carrier to create an open area for the dodger. When the ball carrier approaches a teammate, the teammate cuts through and creates space.

6. *Set a pick for a teammate.* Two teammates can work together by picking and cutting to create a scoring opportunity. If a player cuts off of a pick and does not receive the feed, he rounds out the cut and goes back to his original position to avoid crowding the ball carrier.

7. *Screen the goalie.* When a player is dodging from the midfield, a teammate—usually a crease attackman—screens the goalie to obscure the goalie's ability to see and block a bounce shot.

8. *Exchange places.* Two attackmen or midfielders change places on the field. This simple maneuver occupies defenders and prevents potential defensive slides.

Offensive Team Tactics for Transitional Play

The offensive team's primary objective is to advance the ball to the offensive half of the field and to then work together to create a scoring opportunity. When the goalie, defensemen, or midfielders gain possession of the ball, all players become involved in the transition to offense in an attempt to move the ball from the half of the field they are defending to the half they're attacking.

Many great scoring opportunities arise during the transitional component of the game. Fast-break opportunities and uneven situations create many exciting and productive scoring chances for the offense.

The Fast Break

In the traditional lacrosse fast-break situation, the offense outnumbers the defense four players to three. Three attackmen and a midfielder (or defender) usually carry the ball upfield against three defenders and the goalie. The defense usually slides to the ball carrier. With accurate passing and proper positioning, this situation provides a great chance for a goal.

When the attackmen recognize the four-on-three situation developing, they call out "Fast break," and begin to move away from midline by *angle running* toward their goal. In angle running, the attackers sprint toward their goal while watching the ball carrier.

The attackers (A_1, A_2, A_3) position themselves in an L formation (see figure 11.1) as the ball carrier pushes the ball toward the goal. The ball carrier must be ready to pass the ball when one of the defenders moves toward him to stop his movement to the goal.

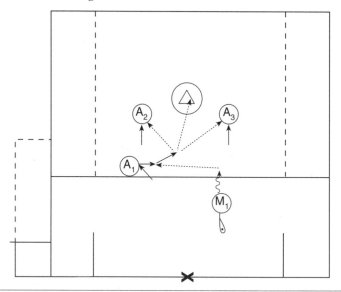

■ **Figure 11.1**   Four-on-three fast break.

When the defenseman commits to the ball carrier, the ball carrier passes the ball to an uncovered attackman. The defense usually will slide from the top, or *point*, attackman, who is positioned at the top of the attack box. The point attackman moves to the pass to position himself in the middle of the cage. If a defender slides to him, he quickly makes another pass. If no defender slides, the attackman goes to the cage and shoots. The original ball carrier stops at the top of the attack box after he has passed the ball. He is the top corner of the offensive box formation and stands ready to receive a pass.

The Slow Break

When the offensive team is in a transitional situation and does not have a clear numerical advantage, the team continues to advance the ball toward its goal by passing. The ball moves much more quickly toward the offensive goal area when players pass than when they run with the ball.

The slow-break pattern attempts to create a scoring opportunity by moving the ball as quickly as possible to the X spot behind the goal and then cutting to the crease area. The slow-break pattern develops best when players pass the ball down the side of the field and then pass to X. Moving the ball quickly to the X spot stretches the defense out and then forces the defense to turn toward the X spot to locate the ball. When the ball arrives at X, midfielders have an opportunity to cut toward the crease. The ball carrier at X then feeds the cutting midfielder for an easy shot. Figure 11.2a identifies a full-team, slow-break pattern. Figure 11.2b shows what can be done when the ball reaches the X spot.

The slow break continues as the remaining midfielders arrive in the offensive half of the field. The midfielder who arrives at the point position first cuts toward X, and the remaining two middies fill in at the top of the attack box to back up any feeds and to be in position to get back on defense if the team loses possession.

The attackmen break to receive the ball in the following pattern: The wing attackman on the ball side breaks out to receive the ball and the opposite wing man breaks to X. The point man always remains in position for the fast break and moves to the opposite wing on the slow break.

This triangle positioning of the attackmen as the ball approaches the offensive half of the field enables them to be in position to react to a fast break and a slow break. The attackman in the offensive half of the field must always be in position to become an outlet for the ball carrier and V cuts to create open passing lanes. The key in transitional offense is for the ball carrier to draw a defender to him and then pass to an open teammate.

In the transitional situation, offensive players continue to pass the ball around the perimeter of the offense looking for cutters before the defense becomes settled. When the defense does become settled, the offense moves from the transitional situation to the settled offense. It is true that transitional situations can create good scoring opportunities, but scoring opportunities

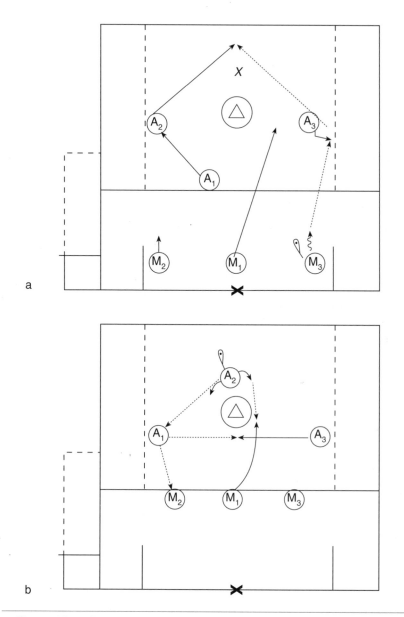

■ **Figure 11.2**   Transition/slow break.

don't always materialize, so a team must know how to handle the ball during its entire offensive possession.

When all potential opportunities for fast-break and slow-break situations have passed, a team flows from its transitional offense to its six-on-six game.

Encourage players to pass the ball, but consider the age, skill, and experience of the players as you coach transitional lacrosse. For example, a player with a weak left hand will most likely cause loss of possession. Since possession of the ball is key, do not put a player without both left- and right-handed passing abilities in a situation that requires these skills. It is crucial to stress passing and stick handling drills during practice. Otherwise, the team will be forced to rely heavily on the players who have both left- and right-handed skills, which creates negative team dynamics.

Offensive Team Drills

Name. Half-Field Fast Break (I/A)

Purpose. To develop offensive and defensive transitional skills and tactics

Organization. Players form one line of attackmen and one line of defensemen. Three attackmen and three defensemen from these lines stand ready just outside the attack box. A line of midfielders stands just inside the midfield line. A goalie is optional for this drill. Roll the ball for one player from the midfield line to scoop; then the player runs the four-on-three fast break. As the fast break begins, the ball carrier or goalie yells "Fast break." The point defenseman yells "Ball," and moves to defend the ball carrier as he crosses the restraining box.

Coaching Points. Watch for the attack and defense to use angle running as they move into the attack box. Remind the offense to set up in an *L* formation, the defense to form a triangle, and both teams to watch the ball as they funnel toward the goal.

Variations. The first player in the attacking line scoops the ball and the first player in the defensive line delays and then chases. This may end in a four-on-four situation.

Name. Half-Field Slow Break (I/A)

Purpose. To develop offensive and defensive transitional skills

Organization. Three attackmen and three defensemen stand just outside the attack box. A goalie is optional for this drill. Two lines of offensive middies position themselves midfield at each wing area. The defensive middies line up in the center of the field, one behind another. Roll or pass the ball to an offensive middie, who runs or passes the ball into his offensive area. The remaining offensive middie also moves toward his goal. The first defensive middie sprints to the defensive box, creating a five-on-four situation.

Coaching Points. Help your team execute these strategies in this drill: The offensive middie scoops the ball and looks to pass immediately ahead to the wing attackman on his side or across to the other middie. Be sure the player passes, rather than runs, the ball. The first defensive middie sprints into the defensive hole area and forms a box with the three defensemen, and the group plays a zone defense until the number of players on each team is even. The offense moves the ball through X, and the first middie into the attack box cuts to receive a feed from the X spot. The second middie stops at the top of the box to provide an outlet and field balance. He will be in position to get back on defense. The offense continues to pass the ball, looking for a good shot.

Variations. Periodically hold the defensive middie to create a five-on-three situation. A second defensive middie delays and sprints into the defensive area, creating a five-on-five situation.

The Six-on-Six Settled Game

When a six-on-six situation exists, all six offensive players must work together to create scoring opportunities. The defense usually focuses on protecting the immediate goal area, and the offense needs a coordinated plan to involve the ball carrier and off-ball players to penetrate the defense.

A sample offense is the 3-1-2, which places two attackmen behind the goal, one on each side; one attackman on the crease; and three midfielders at the top of the attack. This formation provides opportunities for the offense to

- feed and dodge from behind the goal;
- shoot, screen the goalie, and set picks from the crease position; and
- cut and dodge from the midfield positions.

Offensive Options

A number of basic options are available to offensive players who want to initiate a scoring opportunity. Coach all options equally.

The Dodge From Behind

When an attack player (A_1) dodges from behind the goal (see figure 11.3), the adjacent midfielder (M_4) cuts through to create dodging space. The opposite behind attackman (A_2) moves to a position where he can back up a shot. The crease attackman (A_3) moves away from the dodger to a high crease and to the far pipe. The two middies away from the ball (M_5 and M_6) can exchange places. The off-ball movement of these five players occupies defenders and creates an excellent dodging opportunity for the ball carrier.

Cutting and Picking With the Ball Behind

When two attackmen (A_1 and A_2) are handling the ball behind the goal (see figure 11.4), the crease attackman (A_3) can move to a high crease facing the midfielders and set a pick for the midfielders to cut off. He must be ready to

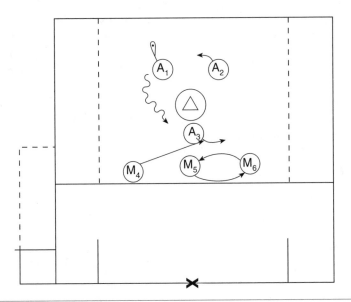

■ Figure 11.3 Dodge from behind.

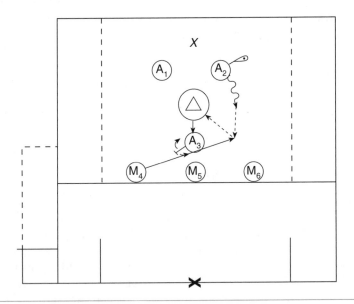

■ Figure 11.4 Cutting and picking.

follow or spin opposite the cutter and become a potential shooter. For example, attackman A_3 sets a pick for midfielder M_4, who cuts to receive a pass from attackman A_2; midfielder M_4 may have a shot opportunity. This movement by the crease attackman and midfielders also creates dodging opportunities for the attackmen behind the goal by occupying off-ball defenders.

> ### *Error Detection and Correction for Team Offense*
>
> Players without the ball must cut through (in toward the crease) when the ball carrier comes toward them to create space. Teach your players never to cut outside the ball.
>
> **ERROR:** Moving outside the ball carrier in the team offense
>
> **CORRECTION**
>
> 1. The player without the ball should cut toward the defender's helmet laces to force the defender to turn and look away from the ball carrier.
> 2. Practice the timing of the cut to maximize offensive opportunities for the ball carrier.

The Midfield Sweep

As shown in figure 11.5, the wing middie (M_1) passes to the center middie (M_2) and cuts to receive a return pass and to create dodging space. The center middie dodges to the vacated area. The crease attackman (A_1) screens the goalie and the two attackmen behind the goal (A_2 and A_3) exchange places as they stand ready to back up a shot. The remaining middie up top (M_3) is in position to get back on defense if the team loses possession.

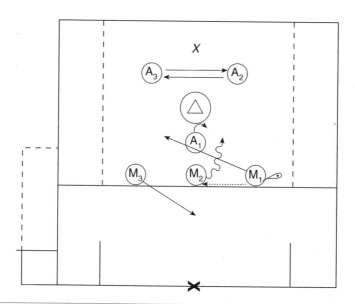

■ **Figure 11.5** Sweep.

Defending in Transition

Transitional situations occur often in a game, and the defense needs a coordinated plan to protect the crease area until the number of defensive players at the crease matches the number of offensive players.

Defending Against the Fast Break

When the defense recognizes that a four-on-three fast-break situation exists, they angle sprint to their defensive goal area and form a tight triangle. The top point of the triangle is five yards inside of the attack box.

As the ball approaches one defender (see figure 11.6), the point man (D_1) slides across to stop the ball. The point man extends out just far enough to force an initial pass. The point man (D_1) must not extend too far from the goal because he must be able to slide back to help defend the player who received the pass. The remaining defenders (D_2 and D_3) slide as subsequent passes are made. By positioning themselves in a tight triangle and reacting quickly to the offense's passes, three defenders can stop the fast break until more defenders arrive.

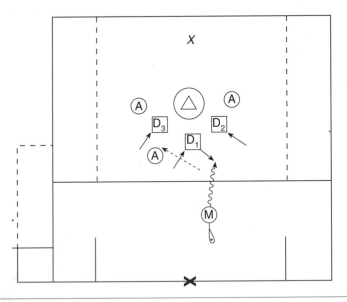

■ **Figure 11.6** Defense fast break.

Midfielders in Defensive Transition

Each midfielder sprints back to his defensive goal area when his team loses the ball. Instruct each player to first get into the hole and then to match up man to man with his offensive opponent. The best way to stop offensive transition is for all six defenders to be in the defensive hole area before the ball arrives.

Six-on-Six Defense

When all six defenders (three defense and three midfield) are in the defensive box area and are matched up man to man on the six offensive players (three attackmen and three midfielders), the defense can coordinate their efforts.

Each off-ball defensive player moves into the hole area and uses the "head on a swivel" technique to constantly look back and forth from the man he is covering to the ball carrier. When the ball carrier gives up the ball, his defender now becomes an off-ball defender and must sink back into the hole area because he does not have to cover his man as tightly when the ball is elsewhere. Then a teammate quickly moves out to the new ball carrier and yells "Ball." The piston motion of one player moving out to play the ball and one pinching in helps to keep the defense from becoming overextended (see figure 11.7).

When the ball is in front of the goal and offensive players are behind the goal without the ball, the off-ball defenders stay above the goal line extended (GLE). No defensive player should go behind the goal to guard a man without the ball, because this prevents him from being in the hole area to provide backup. Instead, he remains just above the GLE until a teammate passes the ball to an attackman behind the goal or until he must slide to cover another player.

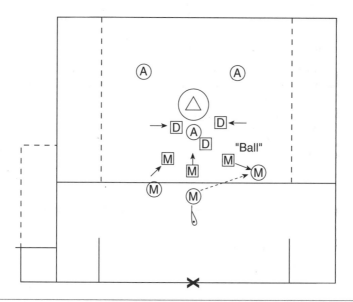

■ **Figure 11.7**   Off-ball defenders pinching in and defending the hole area.

============================== **Transition Drill** ==============================

Name. Seven on Seven (I/A)

Purpose. To develop transitional skills and concepts and overall stick work

Organization. Place the goals at the top of each attack box to shorten the field. Two teams, each consisting of three attackmen, two defensemen, and a goalie, stand around their respective goals. Each team is short one defenseman, which results in a continuous transitional opportunity for the offense. Two midfielders for each team stand across the midfield line. Use offside rules (three players must stay in the defensive half of the field). Each goalie has an ample supply of extra lacrosse balls in the cage, and when a goal or missed shot occurs, the goalie quickly scoops a ball out of the cage and initiates the clear.

Coaching Points. Help the offense and defense recognize fast-break and slow-break opportunities.

Variations. Advanced players carry the ball no longer than four seconds before passing.

Defensive Team Concepts in the Six-on-Six Game

For effective team defense, combine individual skills on and off the ball with these team defensive concepts:

1. *Pressuring the ball.* The defender covering the ball puts pressure on the ball carrier by mirroring his movement with good footwork and by poke checking to disrupt his concentration.
2. *Communicating and providing backup.* Teammates off the ball communicate and provide help if the ball carrier dodges past his defender. Team defense is a collective effort of six players and the goalie. A teammate slides (leaves his man) and moves to stop the ball carrier if the ball carrier has beaten his defender.
3. *Pinching the crease.* When in an off-ball position, five players pinch to the hole area and one player plays the ball carrier on the perimeter.

============================== **Defensive Concepts Drill** ==============================

Name. Five-on-Five Position and Slide (I/A)

Purpose. To teach team defensive concepts

Organization. Five offensive players in the attack box arrange themselves in a 2-1-2 formation with five defensive players matching up on these players. The offensive team passes the ball around the perimeter while you check each player's on-ball and off-ball positioning. Instruct the offensive players not to pass until you have corrected the position of all defensive players.

Coaching Points. Be sure the defensive players use the piston concept as the offensive team passes the ball: One defensive player moves out to the ball and one moves back in. Make sure that the defensive player moves out to the ball in a controlled manner. Otherwise, the ball carrier will simply run past the charging defender and have an open shot. Make sure players understand that if a defenseman runs out, there is no way he can change directions if the ball carrier decides to dodge. Emphasize the pinch concept: Four defenders play in the defensive hole area and one plays the ball outside the hole. Insist on proper defensive communication. Require players to call "Ball" and "Help" on each pass. Listen for the goalie to communicate the location of the ball. Note the position of the crease defender. He must be between his man and the ball at all times. He must play "top side" when the ball is in the midfield and "mask to mask" when the ball is behind. Teach the off-ball defenders to pinch the crease and to continually watch their man and the ball using the "head on a swivel" technique.

Variations. When the ball is in the air on an offensive pass, call "Dodge." To create a slide situation, the defensive player allows himself to be beaten as the ball arrives. Defenders must make correct slides.

Defensive Team Skills

A defense player slides to a dodger if the dodger has clearly beaten a teammate and is within shooting range of the goal. Defensive play requires quick reactions, so all players pinch in toward the crease area with their heads on a swivel.

Slide From the Crease When the Ball Is Up Top

As shown in figure 11.8, when an offensive player (M_1) beats a midfield defender (M_7), a teammate (who is playing between a crease offensive player and the ball) (D_{11}) slides to stop the dodger. An adjacent diagonal defender (D_{12}) slides in to cover the crease. This second slide prevents the easy pass into the crease area.

Slide Across and Down When the Ball Is Behind

When the ball carrier (A_1) beats a defender (D_7) from behind the cage, another defender (D_9) slides across the goal mouth to stop the dodger, and an adjacent player (M_{12}) slides down to cover. The second slide usually comes from a middie (see figure 11.9).

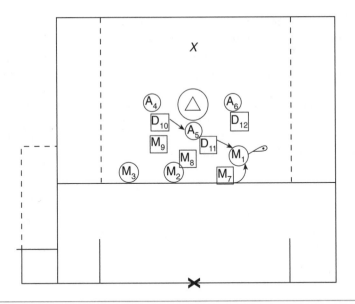

■ Figure 11.8 Slide.

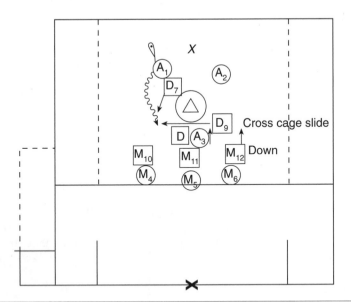

■ Figure 11.9 Slide cross cage by close defender. Midfielder makes second slide.

Communication on Defense

Communication by the defense is critical to success. As each defender's man receives a pass, the defender moves out and yells, "I've got ball." The defender responsible for the initial backup calls, "I've got your help." The second slide defender calls, "I've got two," indicating he has the second slide.

Playing Picks and Cutters

Off-ball defenders call "Pick" to give a teammate time to react to an offensive pick and to slide over the top or behind the pick. Again, communication is important. The man covering the pickman calls a "switch" only if the man playing the cutter is picked off. For example, in figure 11.10, attackman A_9 sets a pick on defender M_4: The off-ball defender M_5 calls "Pick" to alert defender M_4, while defender D_3 calls "Switch" to cover the midfielder M_{10} as he cuts through. Defender M_4 is now responsible for covering attackman A_9.

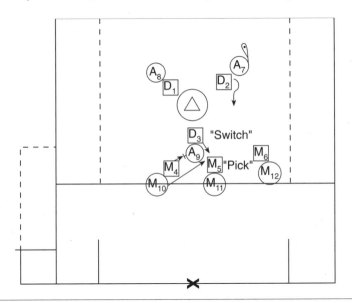

■ **Figure 11.10**   Switch if a teammate is picked off.

Covering a Crease Player

When an offensive player (A_3) positions himself in the hole area directly in front of the goal, the defender (D_9) employs one of several different techniques to defend this immediate scoring threat (see figure 11.11).

When the ball is behind the goal, the crease defender plays face to face with his offensive opponent. He maintains a position between the ball and the offensive player. He holds his stick up straight, ready to check. Holding the stick up straight also enables his teammates to move freely through the crease area without being encumbered by their own crease defender's stick. He does not look for the ball when he's in this position, because any momentary inattention can result in a goal.

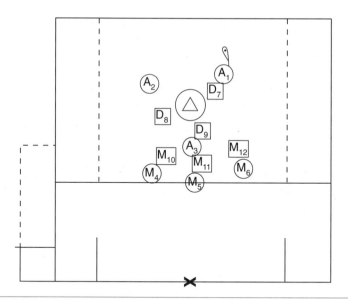

■ Figure 11.11 Face-to-face position on the crease.

When the ball is in the midfield area (see figure 11.12), the crease defender (D_8) again positions himself between the ball and his man. He now keeps his head on a swivel as he acts as the primary backup defender if the ball carrier (M_1) dodges past his teammate (M_{12}) in the midfield. As he quickly looks away from his man to locate the ball, he uses the head of his stick to maintain slight contact with the offensive player. This "topside" position places the defender in good position to slide to a midfield dodger.

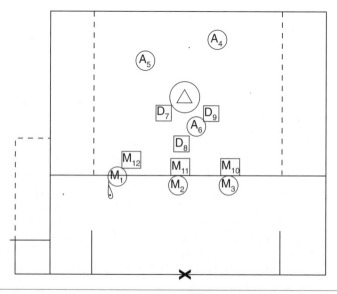

■ Figure 11.12 Topside position of the crease defender.

███████████████ **Passing and Catching Drill** ███████████████

Name. Three-on-Two Grid Passing (A)

Purpose. To develop passing and catching skills under pressure and off-ball movement skills to create passing lanes (for offense); to develop proper stance, breakdown skills, and off-ball peripheral vision (for defense)

Organization. Three offensive players and two defensive players stand within a 15-yard square. The three offensive players pass and move to maintain possession of the ball, while the two defenders apply pressure to force an errant pass or interception. The defenders work in pairs, with one player on the ball carrier and the other splitting the two remaining offensive players. When an offensive player throws the ball, the splitter goes to the ball and the on-ball player becomes the splitter. This simulates the piston movement of team defense. The defenders break down when they move out to the receiver.

Coaching Points. Specify a certain number of passes for the offense to try to complete. Increase or decrease the size of the grid to accommodate different experience levels. Three long-stick players may need a larger grid when trying to maintain possession against two attackers on the defense.

Error Detection and Correction for Team Defense

When sliding on a dodger who has penetrated the defense, the backup (sliding) defender breaks down to a position in which his stick is down and he is partially sitting. If he does not meet the dodger in a body-on-body and stick-on-stick position, he risks being dodged.

ERROR: Failing to establish a good defensive position when sliding

CORRECTION
1. Never lunge at the dodger.
2. Slide in a controlled manner to assure sound defensive positioning.

Clearing

Clearing the ball means advancing the ball from the defensive half of the field to the offensive half. When a team gains possession of the ball in its defensive half of the field, all players become involved in the clear.

The defensive team has a numerical advantage in a clearing situation. The advantage occurs because of the offside rule that requires each team to keep four people in its defensive half of the field and three in its offensive half. With the addition of the goalie, the clearing team has seven players (three defense, three middies, one goalie) and the riding team six players (three attackmen and three middies).

The clearing game comprises the in-bounds clear and the dead-ball clear.

In-Bounds Clear

The in-bounds clear occurs when the ball is in play. It usually results from the goalie making a save or a defender scooping up a loose ball. The team now possesses the ball, and everyone becomes involved in clearing the ball to their offensive half of the field. In this situation, the defensive team instantly moves from defending to attacking.

When the goalie makes a save, he immediately yells "Clear" to let his teammates know that the team has possession and a clear is developing. He looks to immediately pass the ball to the defender who was covering the shooter, because this defender is in position to quickly break out.

The goalie has four seconds in the crease, which allows him ample time to scan the field for an open teammate (see figure 11.13). The midfielders (M_1, M_2, and M_3) break out to the open area between the attack box and the midfield line, looking for an over-the-shoulder pass.

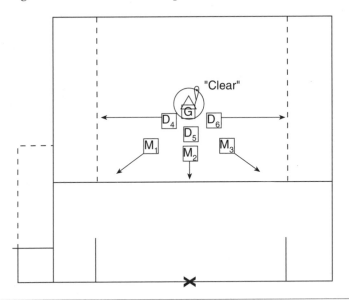

■ **Figure 11.13** Backout by wing defenders on the goalie save.

The wing defender (D_4 or D_6) breaks out on the GLE toward the sideline, watching the goalie at all times. The goalie can safely pass the ball to the wing defender if all midfielders are covered. The defensemen back out with their backs to the sideline.

To protect against a broken clear, the crease defender remains in the hole area until he sees the goalie pass the ball out. When the goalie passes the ball out, the crease defender moves to an open area to receive a pass.

Dead-Ball Clear

The dead-ball clear results when the ball goes out of bounds and an official awards it to the defensive team or when a technical foul awards the ball to the defense. The clearing team spreads the riding team and takes advantage of its seven-on-six advantage.

Dead-ball clears are based on two concepts: to spread the riding team and to create overload situations that place more clearing players than riding players in an area. The three defenders and the goalie position themselves in a line along the goal line extended, while the midfielders spread evenly along the midfield line (see figure 11.14). The goalie has the ball and all players (defenders and midfielders) work together to slowly advance the ball to create a two-on-one situation. A midfielder—who has a shorter stick and therefore better stick handling and ball control abilities—may switch positions with a corner defenseman to increase stick handling on the clear. The ball carrier tries to draw a rider to him and then to advance the ball by passing ahead to an open man. Players off the ball move into open spaces to provide the ball carrier with passing possibilities. Communication is very important. The ball carrier often locates open teammates by hearing their "Help" call.

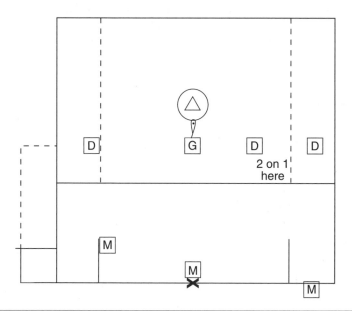

■ **Figure 11.14** Dead-ball clearing pattern.

Riding

Similar to a press defense in basketball or a fore check in hockey, riding involves the six players who have lost possession of the ball in their offensive half and who must now work together to regain possession.

The riding team has only six players (three attack and three midfield) and the clearing team, including the goalie, has seven. Working together, the riders must "hustle" extra hard to compensate for their numerical disadvantage. Much of riding falls on the attackmen, but all midfielders, defensemen, and the goalie have some riding responsibilities.

In an in-bounds ride situation, the attackman closest to the ball immediately goes to the ball carrier and applies pressure. The remaining five riders begin to drop toward their own goal area to defend the open area behind them. Their first priority is to delay the ball from advancing quickly, avoiding a possible fast-break situation.

The two remaining attackmen drop diagonally toward the midfield line and favor the ball side of the field. The attack works together in a triangle zone to regain possession of the ball (see figure 11.15). For example, the goalie yells "Break" and passes the ball to a wing defender (D_1). The crease attackman (A_7) is the closest to the defender (D_1) and rides him. Midfielders (M_4, M_5, and M_6) drop back to get into defensive position. The attackman (A_8) can get into position to create a 2-on-1 situation with A_7 or he can find an opponent to defend.

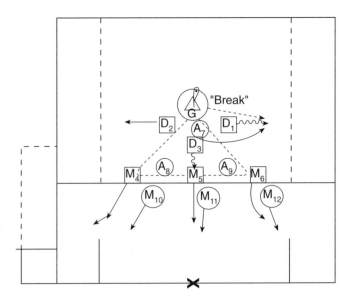

■ **Figure 11.15** In-bounds ride.

As the attackmen work together to regain possession of the ball, the midfielders immediately make the transition to their defensive end. They do not slide up the field to stop the ball, because that may allow the ball carrier to throw the ball over their heads.

The Dead-Ball Ride

A 3-3 zone ride, which places three attackmen and three midfielders in a zone formation covering the area between their attack box and their defensive box, is one of the most basic and effective rides.

The attackmen (A_1, A_2, and A_3) work in a rotating triangle while the three midfielders (M_4, M_5, and M_6) defend one-third of the field in the midfield area (see figure 11.16). In the 3-3 zone, the wing midfielder farthest from the ball (M_4) plays the role of a football free safety and, when the ball is advancing up the side of the field opposite him, drops into his defensive zone area to stop any fast breaks. The attackman who is closest (A_3) must play the defenseman (D_8) that receives a pass from the goalie.

Riding midfielders (M_5 and M_6) do not slide up the field toward the ball carrier unless they can get to a loose ball—or arrive at a pass receiver immediately after the ball does—to dislodge the ball by stick checking or body checking.

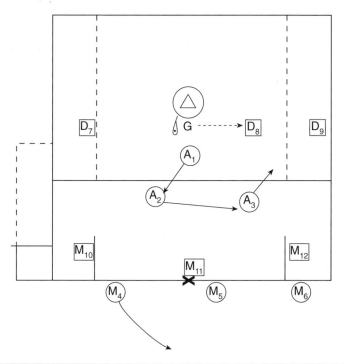

■ **Figure 11.16** 3-3 dead-ball ride.

Error Detection and Correction for Riding

It is important for midfielders to get back on defense when they lose the ball on offense.

ERROR: Midfielders and defensemen who slide up the field to the ball carrier create excessive two-on-one passing situations (a two-on-one passing situation works to the advantage of the clearing team)

CORRECTION

1. Players should play man-to-man defense until the ball carrier is in a critical scoring area.
2. Defensemen need to communicate with each other. For instance, a defensive player should only leave his offender if he has help from a teammate.

Clearing Drill

Name. Four-on-Four With a Neutral Player (I/A)

Purpose. To develop stick skills and riding and clearing tactics

Organization. Remove the goal from the attack box area and position two teams of four players each and a neutral player in the attack box area. The neutral player always plays offense, providing a five-on-four advantage to the team with the ball. Each team tries to maintain possession by running and passing the ball. The defensive team plays zone defense, with one player covering the ball and the remaining three splitting the four remaining offensive players. The offensive players spread the defensive by moving to open areas and calling "Help" when they are open to receive a pass.

Coaching Points. Encourage teams to make quick transitions from offense to defense and from defense to offense as possession changes. Use the goalie as the neutral player to improve his clearing ability.

Variations. Set up two four-on-four neutral drills, one at each end of the field.

Extra-Man Offense

Extra-man offensive situations provide the offense with an excellent scoring opportunity. The offensive team has a one-man advantage, with six offensive players against five defenders and a goalie (who only covers the goal).

Here are the general concepts of the extra-man offense:

1. Select six offensive players to work as an extra-man unit. Teach substitutes for each position the plays and formations.

2. Quickly pass the ball and cut, rather than dodge against the man-down zone defense.

3. Combine simple plays that change the offensive formation with quick passing for good shooting opportunities.

4. Always force a defender to commit to the ball carrier. Each player receives the pass, squares up to the goal, draws a defender to him, and then makes the next pass. Attempt to create a two-on-one advantage.

5. Always have one player in position to back up shots and one player who can get back on defense if the team loses possession.

6. Reverse the direction of the passes often.

7. Be patient. Pass the ball frequently to create a good shot against an organized man-down defense.

8. Have off-ball players cut to receive a pass when the defense focuses only on the ball carrier.

The 2-2-2 Formation

Teach beginning players the 2-2-2 extra-man offensive formation. With all six offensive players positioned on the perimeter, the extra-man offense creates many passing, cutting, and shooting opportunities (see figure 11.17).

The offense passes the ball quickly around the perimeter to create a two-on-one advantage (see figure 11.18). Cutting opportunities for off-ball players arise as teammates pass the ball and defenders focus on only the ball. The

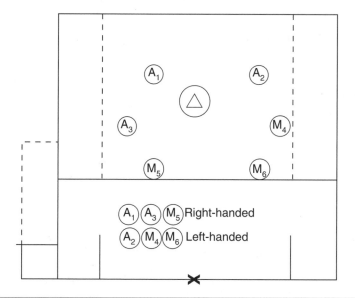

■ **Figure 11.17**   2-2-2 extra-man offensive formation.

off-ball offensive players (A_2, M_4, and M_6) watch the ball and the defenders. For instance, when a defender (M_{12}) turns his back to focus only on the ball, an off-ball offensive player (M_4) cuts to the ball carrier (M_5) for a feed. He circles back to the perimeter if the ball carrier doesn't pass.

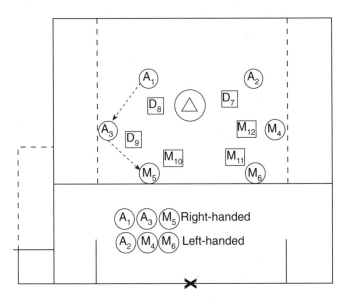

■ **Figure 11.18** The offense passes the ball around the perimeter to create a two-on-one advantage.

The 3-3 Formation

Intermediate players use a 3-3 formation, which positions all players in front of the goal in shooting position. The 3-3 is a good offensive formation for teams that have strong outside shooters. The basic concept in the 3-3 is for the offense to quickly pass the ball around the perimeter to the next open man, always trying to draw a defender. The inside crease player (A_2) continuously moves—as the ball is passed around the perimeter—to receive a pass for an inside shot (figure 11.19). Advanced players may skip pass.

The 1-3-2 and 1-4-1 Formations

Advanced players use the 1-3-2 and 1-4-1 formations. A cutting play begins in a 1-3-2 formation, and players cut into a 1-4-1. This combination affords opportunities for outside shooting and positions a feeder and two inside crease players for inside shooting opportunities.

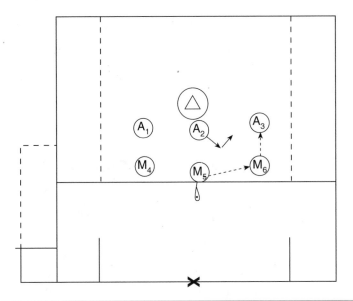

■ **Figure 11.19**   3-3 extra-man offense.

At a predetermined signal (verbal, ball location, or number of passes), the two top middies cut toward the crease and the creaseman moves up to the point position. As the attackman at X receives the ball, he looks for the cutting middies (figure 11.20). The players then shift into a 1-4-1 formation.

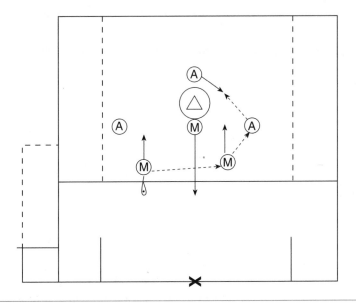

■ **Figure 11.20**   1-3-2 cutting play.

The inside players in the 1-4-1 work together with enough space between each other so one defender cannot cover both players. Players continue to pass the ball around the perimeter as they try to draw a defender and then pass to the open man.

All perimeter players continuously look to the crease for the inside players. The best feeding position is at X. When the ball is behind the cage, the defense must divert its attention from the ball behind to the players in front.

Man-Down Defense Concepts

The man-down defensive unit plays a zone defense to compensate for the extra-player advantage of the offense:

1. Select five defensive players (generally three defenders and two midfielders) to work together as a man-down unit. Prepare two substitutes, one long stick and one midfield, to play if a member of the man-down unit must serve the penalty.

2. The defense works together to protect first against the inside shot and then against the outside shot.

3. Off-ball players sag to the crease to help on the inside.

4. Players who move out to play the ball yell "Ball." Teach players to not extend too far out so they can quickly move back inside when the offensive player passes the ball. The concept of moving out and quickly back is critical in preventing the defense from becoming overextended and creating passing lanes through the zone.

5. Emphasize the pinch concept. As one player moves out to play the ball, the four remaining players pinch into the crease area.

6. Hustle! The defense has one fewer player.

Man-Down Defense

The man-down defense faces the challenge of covering six offensive players with five defenders and a goalie. They must use a zone defense, and each defender must work "double time" to compensate for being a man short. A 2-1-2 zone, similar to a basketball zone defense, is a basic approach to man-down defense (see figure 11.21).

For example, in figure 11.22, midfielder M_4 covers attackman 5M, who passes to attackman 3A, which leaves an attacker (1A) open. Defenseman D_3 must slide across the crease to cover attackman 1A.

Each perimeter player tries to play two offensive players. When none can, the defense slides (rotates) toward the open player in a maneuver similar to the one used in six-on-six defense when a player is beaten.

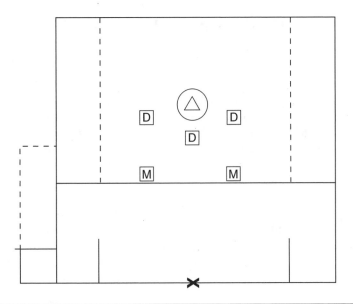

■ **Figure 11.21**   2-1-2 man-down defensive zone.

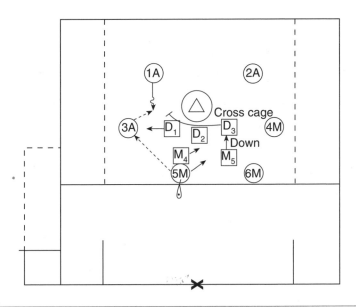

■ **Figure 11.22**   Man-down defense. Defensive rotation (slide) cross cage and down.

Defense Drill

Name. Three-on-Two Scramble (I/A)

Purpose. To develop scooping, passing, shooting, and defensive skills

Organization. Two defensive lines stand behind the goal. The first pair of defenders steps up into the crease area. Three offensive lines stand at the top of the attack box. Roll the ball out for the offense. The three offensive players attempt to create a scoring opportunity against the two defenders and the goalie. Each offensive player who receives a pass tries to draw a defender to him and then passes the ball to the next open man ("draw and dump"). The defense works in pairs, with one player on the ball and one player splitting the other two offensive players. After a pass, the "splitter" goes to the ball and the defender on the ball drops in to become the splitter.

Coaching Points. Expect the offensive players to move the ball quickly when they've gained possession from the ground ball. When the defender drops in to become the splitter, be sure he uses a drop step and watches the ball. Don't let him turn his back on the ball. This drill results in quick transitional situations and gives players practice reacting to riding and clearing opportunities.

Variations. A four-on-three offense works in a box formation around the goal and the defense works in a rotating triangle.

What Is Goalkeeping All About?

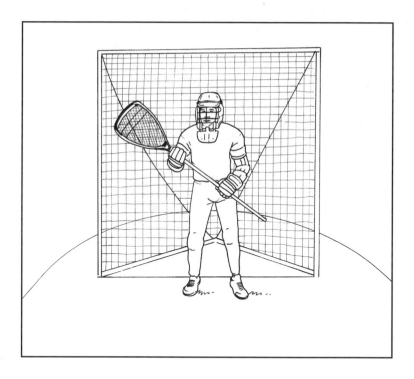

Goalkeeping is the most mentally demanding of all the positions on a lacrosse team. Goalkeepers enjoy the privileges of playing the ball with the hands, playing on the field, and having a crease that is designed especially for them. Goalies also may use an extra-large stick head (it measures 16 inches across at its widest part) to play the ball.

This position needs extra coaching and warm-up because goalies are constantly being shot on, no matter how good the rest of the team is. Goalies are the last line of defense and are constantly pressured to make a big play. They must play with confidence to be successful.

What About Goalkeeping?

An aspiring goalkeeper must have the skills of a good athlete first: speed, quick reactions, and excellent eye-hand coordination. The player should possess very good stick skills and be strong enough to handle the larger and heavier goalkeeper's stick. Most of all, goalies need to be courageous enough to move the stick and body behind each shot. Goalies must also be able to communicate with their teammates throughout the game, while remaining calm, poised, and in control. The ability to concentrate and focus on the ball and the situation on hand is challenging for any young athlete; however, this is also a mental trait to look for and to develop in young goalkeepers.

The Goalkeeper's Team Role

Goalkeepers are leaders on their teams; they are asked to be the "quarterback" of the defense. As goalies develop within a defensive unit, they have an increasing responsibility to communicate to their teammates. The goalkeeper's verbal commands are more extensive in the boys' game, but all goalkeepers must make specific decisions and communicate them to their team. Because goalkeepers are considered the last line of defense, often they are also the players that initiate the attack. Their ability to clear the ball accurately and quickly is key to developing an offensive fast break.

Girls' and Boys' Goalkeepers

The girls' and boys' games of lacrosse differ to some degree, yet they are similar in many ways. The methods and movements of a boys' and girls' goalkeeper to save a shot are very similar. The major differences lie in the pocket size of the shooters' sticks and the release of the shot. Otherwise, major rule differences of the two games, involving the crease and the goalkeeper's privileges, significantly change the goalkeepers' play in certain situations. The skills necessary to be a successful goalkeeper, particularly the method for stopping a shot, are the same in both games. There are, however, a few minor rule differences that govern what a goalie may do with the ball.

Goalkeeper Equipment

A goalkeeper should be properly fitted with protective equipment to prevent serious injury. Major lacrosse manufacturers make goalkeeper equipment in youth sizes. All goalkeepers must wear a helmet with a face mask properly attached. Fit all helmets for the size of the player's head and make sure they have a chin strap and a throat protector. The rules also require goalies to wear a chest pad or a protective upper-body piece. Groin protection for both boys and girls is essential. Recommend that your goalkeepers wear protective equipment for the hands, shins, and thigh areas as well. A soft mesh pocket is recommended for beginners, along with a shorter handle than all other players may choose. See page 61 in unit 6 for an example of goalie equipment.

Where to Start?

First of all, you must spend extra time working with goalkeepers, especially in the beginning. Develop a rapport by encouraging and building the confidence of new goalies. Instruct the players in the fit, use, and care of their equipment. Begin by teaching the ready position, then the body and stick movement toward a shot. Do not throw a ball toward new goalies until they've learned the basic movements. Consider teaching goalkeeping skills by having the player follow or shadow you as you go through the basic movements, starting with the feet then moving to the hips, shoulders, head, and finally the stick.

Goalkeeper Skills

Young goalkeepers need a high level of inspiration and positive influences. Developing the fundamental goalkeeping skills gives young goalies a solid base. In your instruction, emphasize the development of both the mental and physical skills of goalkeeping.

Ready Position

The ready position should be the home base for every goalie just before he or she makes a save. A good ready position in the goal is a lot like the ready position of the middle linebacker in football. The keeper stands with hips square to the ball carrier, hands always away from the body, and a strong focus on the ball. No matter how much movement the goalkeeper may be required to make during play, a coach should emphasize the need to be ready or set to receive a shot.

Goalies in the ready position stand with their feet shoulder width apart, weight on the balls of the feet, and toes pointed toward the shooter (see figure 12.1). They remain balanced at all times, while leaning slightly forward with their knees and hips slightly flexed. The head stays level, with the eyes focused on the ball. The arms extend partially, holding the stick away from and diagonally across the body, with the dominant hand positioned at the uppermost part of the shaft. The grip rotates slightly to the right, or counterclockwise, so the goalie can move the stick to the opposite shoulder without changing the grip. A young goalie must not squeeze the shaft; the tighter the grip, the slower the reaction speed. Stress the idea of "soft" hands.

■ **Figure 12.1** Goalie ready position.

Teach goalies these skills so they will execute the ready position correctly:

1. Grasp the stick at the base of the head.
2. Keep arms extended away from the body and on a diagonal.
3. Put the top hand at shoulder level, the bottom hand at waist level.
4. Flex the knees and hips, and be ready to move.

The Save

The key to making a save on a shot is to track, or see, the ball all the way into the stick head. We present several visual ball drills later in the warm-up drills section (beginning on p. 231). Incorporate them into your daily practice to improve eye tracking skills. After your goalies can see the ball in flight, teach them how to move their stick and body in a position to keep the ball from going past them.

Feet

Be sure you teach goalkeepers to move toward the ball as it is released by stepping to one side on a 45-degree angle toward the ball (see figure 12.2). This step is toward the side of the goalie that the ball is heading. For example, if the ball is coming to the right side of the goalie, then the goalie steps with the right foot. The toe of the lead foot points to the shooter. Discourage the goalie from pointing the toe toward the sideline and opening up the hips. The weight should transfer to the lead foot as the trail foot moves next to the lead. The feet should never come together; goalies should strive always to bring the trail foot back parallel to the lead foot to enable the hips to remain square to the shooter.

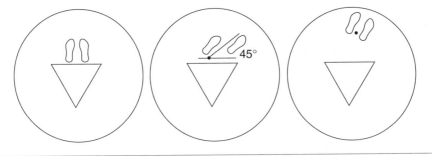

■ **Figure 12.2** Goalie's feet position when moving toward a ball.

Teach goalies these footwork skills for executing a save:

1. Step on a 45-degree angle toward the ball.
2. Transfer weight to the lead foot from a balanced position.
3. Keep the toe pointing at the shooter.
4. Bring feet back side by side in a parallel stance after the save to close up the space between the legs.

Body

Because the body provides a back-up to the stick in making a save, goalies try to position as much body area behind the shot as possible. A forward step at a 45-degree angle to the ground initiates this body movement. The shoulders and hips move together behind the shot and remain square to the shooter. If a shot hits the ground and bounces upward, goalies must keep the upper body leaning forward slightly to keep the rebound in front of them (by bending at the knees more than at the waist).

To position their body correctly during a save, goalies follow these instructions:

1. Align the shoulders with the hips to remain square to the shot, and stay over the lead foot.
2. Bend at the knees instead of the waist and lower the center of gravity to save a low shot.

Stick

If goalkeepers hold the stick in the correct position when they're ready to receive a shot, then the only movements necessary are to move the stick behind the shot and to give with the shot. Basically, the arms move the stick to the correct position and the top hand, wrist, and arm give with the shot to keep the ball in the stick pocket. Often, beginners are tempted to reach or to push the stick head at the ball, which creates a hitting motion. Remind players to give with the ball as it reaches the mesh pocket. Emphasize that a good goalie is simply trying to block the ball.

The stick moves within a plane that is parallel to the shoulders and hips, but that is 8 to 14 inches away from the body. (The distance from the body depends on what is comfortable for the goalie.) In any movement of the stick, the hands do not move toward or away from the body (see figure 12.3, a-c). The top hand guides the stick head to meet the ball in front of the body as the body moves forward with a step. The stick head travels a straight line from the set position to the save position and it doesn't rotate around the body.

Goalies execute these steps with their stick during the save:

1. Give with the arms, wrists, and hands to keep the ball in the stick's pocket.
2. Keep both hands in front of the body to move the stick head directly behind the shot.

Ground Shots

Shots that hit the ground in front of the goalkeeper are often the most difficult to receive. As you teach the positioning for all shots, emphasize how to play a ground shot. If a shot hits the ground and bounces upward, the goalie needs to keep the upper body leaning forward from the waist

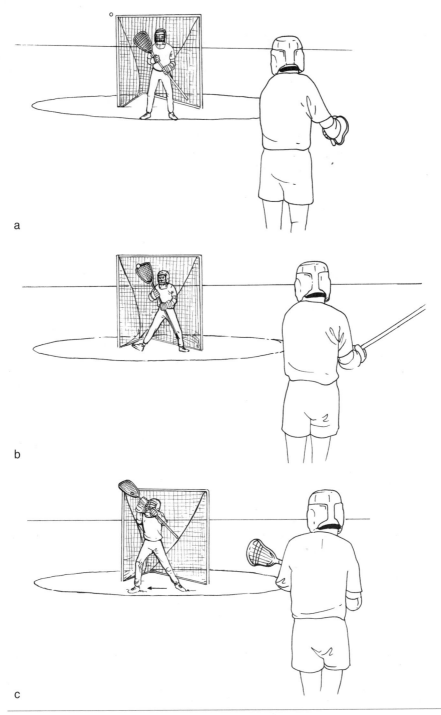

a

b

c

■ **Figure 12.3** Goalie stick position on a high shot save.

to keep any rebound in front of the goalkeeper. Teach goalies to lower their center of gravity or to squat, rather than just bending at the waist, as the bounce shot approaches. Squatting allows them to see the ball and to react to any crazy bounce. It also allows the goaltenders to react to rebounds.

The stick moves to an inverted position of the ready position when the shot is released: that is, the left hand over and the right hand below for right-handed goalkeepers. Once the stick is inverted, it angles away from the body, so that the left hand is extended farther out from the body than the right. This traps the ball (see figure 12.4, a-b).

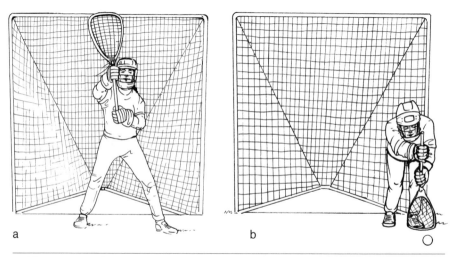

a   b

■ **Figure 12.4**   Goalie stick position on a bounce shot.

Only after goalies understand and have practiced these foot, body, and stick movements without a ball coming toward them should you begin to throw a ball to represent a shot. Throw a lot of balls to a specific area to develop a pattern of correct movement with a young goalie (see warm-up drills beginning on p. 231).

Positioning Within the Crease

After goalies have the proper technique to save a shot from a stationary shooter, they must begin to understand the importance of angles relative to their positioning in front of the goal. It is important to teach goalies to align their body position off of the stick of the shooter, not off the shooter's body. When a ball carrier changes hands from left to right as he looks to shoot, the goalkeeper makes a small, but very necessary, adjustment to his or her positioning to reduce the player's angle for a shot. Teach all goalkeepers the theory of stepping up on a shot to reduce the available scoring area.

As a ball carrier moves across the goal mouth, the goalkeeper moves to maintain the angle in the middle of the shooting space. Visually check after each shot to see that the goalkeeper has covered the shot with equal space to either side. Although the goalie takes smaller steps than a field player circling the cage does, the steps must be quick, balanced, and precise to maintain good body positioning. These small lateral steps allow the goalie to be ready to step toward the shot at any time.

One common method of helping youngsters understand the correct positioning within the crease is called the *house method*. Outline a house on the ground for the goalkeeper's feet to follow (see figure 12.5). If the shooter is in the middle of the field, then the goalie will be at the peak of the roof. If the shooter is level with the goal line, then the goalkeeper will be on the post (pipe), or at ground level of the house. The goalkeeper stands where the roof meets the side wall of the house if the shooter is on a 45-degree angle halfway between center and goal line. In practice, begin to shoot on your goalies only after they know by sense and visual memory their way around the cage without looking down at their feet.

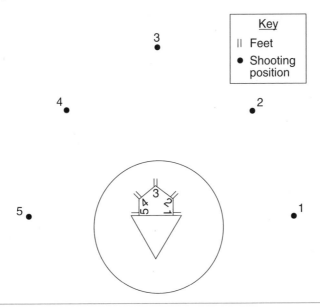

■ Figure 12.5   The house method of positioning within the crease.

Another common approach to helping goalkeepers understand movement is the *arc method*, which allows goalies to stay closer to the pipes. In the arc method, goalies create an imaginary arc that goes from one pipe to the other and follows the same path as the crease. They try to keep their heels on the arc as the ball moves around up top. The top of the arc should be 12 to 18 inches from the goal line (see figure 12.6). Picturing an arc that goes from pipe to pipe is very simple for young players.

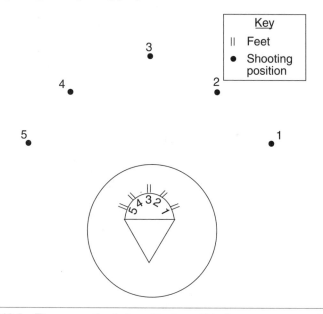

■ **Figure 12.6**   The arc method of positioning within the crease.

When a player passes the ball to a teammate in front of goal, the goalkeeper moves while the ball is in the air and tries to be set in the new alignment when the opposing player catches the ball. Remind goalkeepers to always "see the ball in the air," and with practice they will learn to position themselves in the correct angle as they move.

The most difficult situation for a goalkeeper to defend is a pass from behind the cage to a player in front. Instruct the keeper to drop step the foot that's on the same side as the shoulder the ball is moving past. The drop step allows the hips to rotate around and the goalie to step up to the new position (see figure 12.7, a-c). When the ball is directly behind the goal, the keeper moves to the middle of the house with the head of the stick up over the top of the goal cage to intercept any pass over this area. The goalkeeper increases his or her reach by pushing the butt of the stick held with the bottom hand up through the top hand. Warn young goalkeepers against becoming tempted to overcommit themselves to intercept a pass; they'll be left way out of position for defending the shot if the interception is unsuccessful.

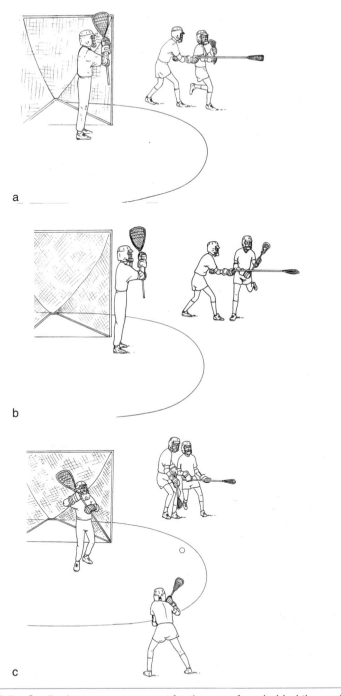

a

b

c

■ Figure 12.7   Goalie drop step movement for the pass from behind the goal.

Play Outside the Crease

On some occasions, the goalkeeper must come out of the crease to play the ball or an opponent. If she or he makes a mistake in decision-making, the opponents usually score. However, nothing is more enjoyable and exciting for a goalkeeper and the team than the goalkeeper intercepting a pass on the field and starting a fast break.

A goalie proficient in ground-ball pickups is an asset to the team, because any loose ball that she or he can get to and play first results in a possession. On a fast break against a goalkeeper, the opposing team is taught to slide and pressure the ball, which results in an extra, unmarked opponent close to the goal. An experienced goalie seizes that opportunity to intercept the last pass to the free player. Often the goalkeeper plays a shooter who is very close to the crease by stepping forward and blocking the ball as it comes out of the shooter's stick. With further experience, a goalie may choose to come out of the crease and check the ball carrier in a surprise tactic. A common mistake that a young goalie makes, however, is to be too quick to leave the goal. Constantly remind your goalie to be a goalie first and a field player second.

Clearing the Ball

A goalkeeper should be able to handle the stick in such a way as to dodge opponents and throw a clearing pass while on the move. Instruct the young goalie how to throw with the extra-large stick, because the technique is different than throwing with a regulation field stick and the goalie needs more time and space to prepare the stick for the throw. Instruct the players to take the head of the stick back behind and above the throwing arm's shoulder. From here, the stick head travels up and then out to the target. Often goalies have more success if they slide the top hand down the shaft about six inches.

The boys' and girls' games differ significantly in the goalkeeper's privileges and time of possession. In the following paragraphs, we summarize the rules and how they affect the goalkeeper's role in clearing the defensive end of the field.

Clearing Strategies in Girls' Lacrosse

A goalkeeper in the girls' game may use her hands while playing a ball in her crease. After the ball enters the crease, she has 10 seconds to remain in this area and look for a pass to a teammate. By the end of the 10-second count, she must have passed the ball or moved outside of the crease where an opponent may check her. She may, however, roll the ball back into the crease to accrue another 10 seconds to decide what to do with the ball.

Your goalkeeper's throwing ability determines what options are available for your team. Young goalies may not have enough upper-body strength or accuracy to throw the ball very far. Therefore, coach your defensive unit on making short passes and controlling the ball up the field. If a goalkeeper can pass accurately over 30 yards or more, the team has the option to go for a longer clear directly to the attack.

Clearing Strategies in Boys' Lacrosse

After the goalie makes a save, he has four seconds before he needs to vacate the crease. Remind young goalies that four seconds is a long time. Teach him not to rush the pass or to run the ball out of the crease into traffic. Teach your goalie this four-point checklist for clearing:

1. Always look to where the shot came from. The defensive players should have a step on the offense, so try to push the transition.
2. Look high and away first; if you determine the first look is not there, look to the other midfielders, who are breaking upfield.
3. Look to your wing defensemen. By now, the count should be two and a half seconds. Find an open teammate that you feel confident you can get a pass to.
4. Look for a safe alley to leave the crease. If everyone is covered, then the goalie is the open player. In this case, find a safe way to leave the crease.

Here are some key coaching points:

- The pass to the crease defenseman in the middle of the field is a risky pass; discourage it.
- Count out loud to help the goalie learn to keep possession for at least three and a half seconds. Young goalies usually force the clear in two and a half seconds. Four seconds is really cutting it close.

Goalkeeper Teaching Progression

The goalkeeping position combines a range of challenging skills for a young player. When teaching them, start with and allow your goalies to master the most fundamental and easy skills first. This allows the goalies' confidence to build and provides a solid base from which to progress.

Spot Shooting

Teach the goalkeeper the proper body and stick positioning for each of the following areas. Concentrate on correcting the technique in one area before you move on to the next. Use a high repetition of tosses or shots to imprint correct movement for each area of the goal.

1. High right
2. High left
3. Middle right
4. Middle left
5. Low right
6. Low left
7. Bounce shots
8. Between the feet
9. Anywhere

Use this progression to warm up the body. Low shots are the toughest to get to, so they should come later in the warm-up. Shoot 10 to 15 shots at each spot before moving to the next. Make up games toward the end of warm-up. Challenge your goalie to save 70 percent of your tosses.

Make sure that goalies, especially younger ones, are in the ready position before each shot. Teach this trick to help goalies with ball saving: Make an imaginary line from the belly button to the nose and try to split the ball in half with that line each time a shot is taken. If the goalie turns the hips, it will be impossible to split the ball in half. If the ball is shot to the goalie's left, the whole body must move to split the ball.

Angles Around the Cage

After the goalie has gone though spot shooting, instruct your goalkeepers about the importance of maintaining the correct angle to best defend and save a shot. Demonstrate how the body's angle works by tying to each post a rope that reaches out about 8 to 10 yards from the cage. As you walk around an arc with the rope pulled tightly around a stick shaft, your goalkeepers can visualize the cone-shaped area they must cover and they can see how one step to the left or right will cover the angle of a shot to that post. When the goalkeepers see the scoring space to either side, they transfer this visual cue into a feeling of being in the center of a shot on goal.

When the goalies understand the concept of positioning themselves for angle shots, begin to shoot at them. When shooting at an angle, stay stationary during the shot, but move to a different spot on the arc after each shot. Before each shot, give feedback on the keepers' positioning ("Right side open," "Middle [good]," "Left side open"). Only after your keepers have learned to align correctly with a stationary shooter may they move before a shot.

Movement Before the Shot

The next step in the teaching progression is for the goalkeeper to move around the cage with the player before taking the shot. The simplest movement is straight across the goal or parallel to the goal line. Instruct goalkeepers to move in small, quick steps around the "arc" or "house," keeping their shoulders square to the shooter. Also remind the keepers to stay balanced on the toes of both feet so they can be set and ready to step with either foot to make a save. To help goalies develop skills for defending from different distances and angles of approach to the cage, you can also switch top hands on the stick to change the location of the shot.

Shot From a Pass

The next skill to teach young goalkeepers is how to move and position when an attacker passes to a teammate who then shoots at goal. In this situation, two players or coaches position themselves in front of the cage and pass a ball between them. Upon each catch, the player looks to shoot, checking the angle and set position of the keeper. Only after goalkeepers feel comfortable that they know where they are in the crease after each pass should a shot follow a catch. Eventually, change the shooters' location in front of goal between each pass or after every shot.

Defending a Pass From Behind

Goalkeepers who are trying to defend a pass from behind and are trying to save a shot from in front of the goal should be instructed about correct movements of the feet, body, and stick. First teach the proper footwork of turning as an opponent passes the ball over the cage: To rotate efficiently, the goalie pivots to the side over which the ball is passed, then steps up with the trail foot (see figure 12.7 on page 227). Make the goalies repeat the footwork to imprint the skill so they can immediately react to the ball's movement. Next teach keepers how to read the pass and to position on the turn so they arrive on the correct angle to save the shot. Finally, show them how to extend, or telescope, the stick through the top hand to try to intercept the pass. Remember to discourage keepers from jumping to try for an interception over the cage.

Goalkeeper Warm-Up

Goalkeepers need extra time and attention to prepare before other players shoot on them. Develop a warm-up routine to teach, supervise, and encourage young goalkeepers before they step into the crease. These routines help warm up the goalkeepers' body and improve their balance, conditioning, and concentration. We've outlined several warm-up suggestions in the following section, but there are many more possibilities. The goalkeepers should be fully dressed in all their equipment to practice these movements.

Daily Practices

To be successful, young goalkeepers must acquire agility, balance, confidence, quick reactions, and leadership. Practicing such skills as footwork, stick control, and body positioning daily will help goalies develop mentally and physically.

Footwork

Goalkeepers must be prepared to move quickly from one place to another within the crease. First, young goalies should develop speed and then gain knowledge of how and where to step.

Here are some footwork activities:

➡ *Over and Around the Stick (B).* The goalkeeper's stick is on the ground. The goalkeeper steps, with one foot following the other, over and back across the shaft of the stick as quickly as possible (see figure 12.8a). Each time the goalie steps over the stick with both feet, the feet should be in the ready position. Next, starting at the bottom of the shaft with toes perpendicular to the shaft, shuffle sideways toward the head. When you reach the top of the head, run forward to the other side of the head; then, with your back toward the stick, shuffle sideways back to the end of the stick (see figure 12.8b). Finally, starting at the bottom of the shaft and facing the stick head, run forward to the top of the stick, shuffle sideways across the basket, and run backward to return to the bottom of the shaft (see figure 12.8c). Make as many trips around the stick as you can in 15 seconds.

➡ *Box Drill (B).* Form a cross with two sticks on the ground. The goalkeeper moves from one corner of the box to the next. The keeper gets into the ready position with each move to a new corner (see figure 12.9a). The goalie may step only with the inside foot when changing boxes. Establish various patterns or changes of direction (see figure 12.9b)

Stick

Young goalkeepers must orient themselves with the stick. Learning how to hold the stick, how to move the stick, and how to throw with the stick are all skills needed to save a shot on goal.

Here are some stick-work activities:

➡ *Quick Stick (B).* Stand with a ball about five yards away from the goalkeeper. Toss the ball underhanded to the goalkeeper's right shoulder. The goalkeeper steps forward with the right foot as he or she watches the ball enter the stick and gives with the catch. The goalkeeper returns

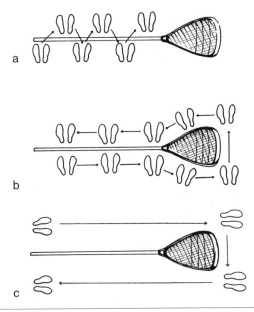

■ **Figure 12.8** Goalie footwork activities: Over and Around the Stick.

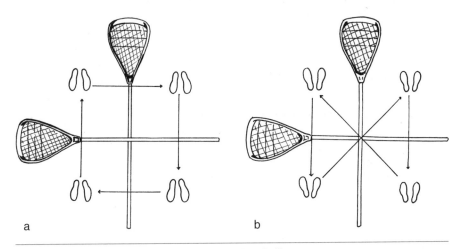

■ **Figure 12.9** Goalie footwork activities: Box Drill.

the ball to you in a quick-stick motion after the give. Back up one step as the goalkeeper advances one step on each throw. Emphasize the step to the ball and the give with the catch.

Variations. Toss to different areas of the goalkeeper's body. Toss the ball from alternate hands so the goalkeeper has to locate and then track the ball. Increase speed of delivery of the toss (not speed of the throw).

➡ *Spot Shadow Tag (B)*. The goalkeeper stands where he or she has space to move forward. The goalkeeper makes five imaginary saves to each area, returning to a ready position between each. For example, the goalie makes five saves to high right, to middle right, to low right, between feet, overhead, to high left, to middle left, and to low left. Emphasize correct technique and stick, feet, and body movement.

Variations. You call the spot for the goalkeeper to save to. The goalkeeper makes one save to each area five times through the cycle. The goalie turns 180 degrees before making the imaginary save.

Body

The goalie always starts with the body in the ready position. The body position changes according to the location of the ball on the field. A goalkeeper keeps the body between the goal and the ball.

Here are some body position activities:

➡ *Step Up (I/A)*. Use the same setup as in Quick Stick, except the goalkeeper doesn't use a stick. The goalkeeper steps to the ball and catches with two hands together, trying to move the body behind the ball. Emphasize stepping to the ball, keeping the toes pointing toward coach, and keeping the shoulders and hips square behind the ball.

Variations. Toss the ball with alternate hands. Decrease time between throws. Add fakes.

➡ *Circle the Cage (I/A)*. The goalkeeper stands in the crease near one post. Move along an arc about 10 yards from one post to the other and back. While looking out toward you, the goalkeeper moves around the crease, following the house. Emphasize moving at the speed of the coach; keeping shoulders and hips square; making small, quick steps; and staying balanced and in the ready position at all times. Check angles as the goalkeeper moves.

Variations. Change speed and direction of the tosses or change the hand you throw with. Add fake shots to see if the goalie is set. Set up a pass from behind to check the goalkeeper's turning and angles.

After the preliminary warm-up, a goalkeeper should then continue to warm up with shots from a coach or trained player. The object is to allow the goalkeeper enough time and practice in making saves in a controlled environment. Begin with shots at about 50-percent speed, and increase as the warm-up routine continues. Don't progress in the warm-up until the goalkeeper feels comfortable at the speed you're using or with the drill. The goalkeeper must concentrate on seeing the ball out of the shooter's stick and into his or her own stick as the speed of the shots increases. Never allow your own or a player's ego to interfere with the warm-up of the goalkeeper. In other words, don't make scoring on a shot an objective as you help the goalie warm up.

Progress daily in the warm-up as in the teaching progression. Don't add players to a goalie's warm-up drills until the goalie is ready. Remember to instruct the players that their purpose is to help warm up the goalkeeper; it's not to let loose and shoot uncontrollably. Be sure to include the skills of throwing and clearing for a goalkeeper at some point in the warm-up.

Goalie Drills

Name.   Rapid Fire (I)

Purpose.   To practice seeing the ball and reacting to a quick shot

Organization.   Arrange 6 to 12 players in a semicircle around the goal approximately 10 yards from the crease. Each player should have several balls. Assign each player a number and have the players stay in that order around the circle unless you instruct otherwise. Tell the players and the goalkeeper the shooting pattern they will complete. Signal with a whistle when to start and when to release the next shot.

Coaching Points.   Be sure shooters follow your commands of where and when to shoot. Control the time between each shot with a whistle or verbal command. Always start with the easiest variations and progress to the more challenging ones after the players experience success. Be sure goalkeepers get an adequate rest between sets of shots, or rotate the rounds with another goalkeeper.

Variations.

Shot Heights (I). Instruct shooters to limit shots to high, low, bounce, or middle. Have odd-numbered players shoot low and evens shoot high.

Shooter's Location (I). Instruct the shooters to shoot in a specific order: 1 to 10, 10 to 1, inside out (6, 5, 7, 4, 8, 3, 9, 2, 10, 1), outside in (1, 10, 2, 9, 3, 8, 4, 7, 5, 6). Each of these changes in order will drill the goalkeeper to move in different directions.

Find the Shot (A). Players stand in any order around the crease. Call out numbers in order 1 to 10, but shots come from anywhere around the arc. Instruct each shooter to make a specific movement before the shot so the goalkeeper can find where the next shot is coming from, then reduce the time between when you call the number and when the shooter shoots. Have players toss the ball to themselves before a shot. Progress to shooters having their backs to the goal cage, turning, then shooting. Finally, allow shooters just one cradle before a shot.

Turn and Shoot (A). The goalkeeper faces the back of the cage. As you call a number, the goalkeeper completes a drop step to turn around and face the shot from a player. Progress from having players toss to themselves before a shot to a more rapid release of the shot.

Name.   Clearing From a Shot (I)

Purpose.   To teach goalkeepers how to make the transition from saving a shot to initiating the attack

Organization.   Stand 8 to 10 yards in front of the goal cage with a lot of balls. The goalkeeper stands in the crease ready to receive a shot from you. Arrange other players in groups of four. The first set of four players steps up between you and the crease. As you release the shot, the players watch to see if the goalkeeper saves the shot. If the goalkeeper saves the ball (it's in the stick), the players break out from the crease area and position themselves to cut to receive a pass from the goalkeeper (see figure 12.10). After the goalkeeper's first pass to a side of the field, the players continue to cut, catch, and pass upfield until all the players receive the ball at least once. If the shot rebounds out of the crease, the players chase the ball and return it to the goalkeeper to begin the clear upfield.

Coaching Points.   Instruct the goalkeepers to concentrate on making the save first before beginning to clear the ball. Also have the goalkeepers step to one side of the cage or the other to throw the ball so the ball won't roll out of the stick and into the goal. Encourage the goalkeeper to practice throwing to all possible cutters and to follow the first pass out of the crease to be ready for a return pass.

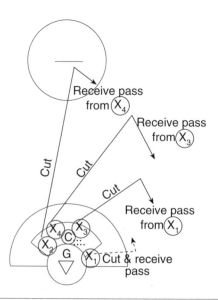

■ **Figure 12.10**   Clearing From a Shot Drill.

Variations.

Goalkeeper (A). Vary the types of shots to create rebounds. Try spinning the ball or tossing it into the air near the crease to create a decision-making situation for the goalkeeper and field players. Also practice defensive communication for covering a shot that misses the cage.

Players (A). Vary the position the players must start from, (i.e. two behind the cage and two in front, all four on their knees, two by the crease and two behind the coach). Tell the players what type of cuts are allowed or what type of passes to use (e.g., direct cuts to the ball only, only sidearm passes, catch and roll as you change hands to pass).

Name. Six Shooter (A)

Purpose. To practice goalkeeper's rapid movement around the crease and making a save

Organization. This drill is excellent for teaching goalkeepers to concentrate and move. Arrange six to eight players in specific spots around the crease. Instruct the players and goalkeeper as to the order and type of shots to release. On your signal, players make these shots:

1. Stationary center shot (allow only one step)
2. Feed from right corner across goal to shooter 2 (allow only one step)
3. Player from behind left carries the ball to one step in front of goal line and shoots.
4. Feed from left corner across goal to shooter 4 (allow only one step)
5. Player from behind right carries ball to one step in front of goal line and shoots.
6. Stationary center shot (allow only one step)

Coaching Points. Watch the goalkeepers' movements and signal when the next shooter or feeder should begin. Allow little delay between all six shooters but adequate rest between sets of six shots. Remind goalkeepers of the pattern: shot, pass, shot, crease shot, pass, shot, crease shot, shot; or repeat the side movements: center, right to left, left to right, center. Suggest the goalkeepers go through the progression of movements in the pattern before any shots are released. Watch for efficient movement, stick positioning, and covering of shooting angles.

Variations.

Number of Players (A). Use the same player to do two shots (e.g., one player could shoot shots 1 and 6 or 3 and 5). Challenge the crease from each side. Have fewer shooting stations (but we recommend having no more than six in a set for beginners).

Change the Pattern (A). Switch the order of shots to have goalkeepers move in the reverse direction (i.e., switch 2 with 4 and 3 with 5). Add a pass from behind instead of using a crease shot.

Name. Ground Ball and Throw (A)

Purpose. To teach goalkeepers to move out of the crease to field a loose ball and make a pass to a teammate

Organization. This drill works well with up to four goalkeepers rotating in from behind the goal cage. Stand three to five yards in front of the crease with balls. Arrange a line of players behind you. Roll or bounce a ball toward the crease. One goalkeeper runs out to pick up the ball and continues to run to a side of the field away from the goal cage while getting the ball under control in the stick. As soon as the goalkeeper moves to one side or the other of the goal mouth, the first player in line cuts to the same side as the goalkeeper to receive a pass.

Coaching Points. Instruct the goalkeepers to verbally call for the ball as they make the decision to come out of the crease to play the ball. Advise the goalkeepers to run through the ball and to continue out to a side of the field, not up the middle. Encourage proper technique with the stick and body while picking up the ball, cradling, dodging, and throwing. Warn the goalkeepers to react to the ball and not to anticipate what the coach may do.

Variations.

Coach (A). Vary the roll or toss of the ball to include different angles, speeds, spins, bounces, and fakes. Place a time limit on the goalkeeper ("You have only two seconds to pass the ball," or, "You must hold the ball in control for eight seconds.")

Pressure Player (A). Add a player or two, positioned in different places around the crease, to pressure the goalkeeper as soon as he or she steps out of the crease to field the ball. Try starting the player behind or to the side of the crease as well as in front.

Appendix A

Sample Season Plan for Beginning Girls' Lacrosse Players

Goal: To help players learn and practice the individual skills and team tactics needed to play a lacrosse game successfully.

T(#) = Initial skill teaching time (minutes)   * = Skills practiced during drills and activities

P(#) = Review and practice time (minutes)

Skills	Week 1 Day 1	Week 1 Day 2	Week 2 Day 1	Week 2 Day 2	Week 3 Day 1	Week 3 Day 2	Week 4 Day 1	Week 4 Day 2
Warm-Up Exercises**	T(10)	P(10)	P(10)	P(10)	P(10)	P(10)	P(10)	P(10)
Cool-Down Exercises	T(5)	P(5)	P(5)	P(5)	P(5)	P(5)	P(5)	P(5)
Evaluation	(5)	(5)	(5)	(5)	(5)	(5)	(5)	(5)
Fundamentals								
Player positions	T(5)	Reviewed daily.						
Field rules	T(5)	These will be emphasized during drills and scrimmages.						
Cradling								
Strong side	T(5)	P(5)	*	*	*	*	*	*
Weak side	T(5)	P(5)	*	*	*	*	*	*
Nondominant side	T(5)	P(5)	*	*	*	*	*	*
Throwing								
Dominant side	T(5)	P(5)	*	*	*	*	*	*
Nondominant side	T(5)	P(5)	*	*	*	*	*	*
Shovel pass			T(5)	P(5)	*	*	*	*

**Athletes do additional warm-up before the official practice warm-up session begins.

Skills (continued)	Week 1		Week 2		Week 3		Week 4	
	Day 1	Day 2	Day 1	Day 2	Day 1	Day 2	Day 1	Day 2
Ground Ball Pickups	T(5)	P(5)	*	*	*	*	*	*
Catching								
Strong side	T(5)	P(5)	*	*	*	*	*	*
Wrap catch	T(5)	P(5)	*	*	*	*	*	*
Give catch	T(5)	P(5)	*	*	*	*	*	*
Nondominant side	T(5)	P(5)	*	*	*	*	*	*
Over the shoulder				T(5)	P(5)	*	*	*
Dodging								
Roll dodge		T(5)	P(5)	*	*	*	*	*
Pull dodge		T(5)	P(5)	*	*	*	*	*
Change-of-hands dodge		T(5)	P(5)	*	*	*	*	*
Shooting								
Inside		T(5)	P(5)	*	*	*	*	*
Outside		T(5)	P(5)	*	*	*	*	*
On the run		T(5)	P(5)	*	*	*	*	*
Quick stick							T(5)	P(5)
Picking					T(5)	P(5)	P(5)	P(5)
Body Checking				T(5)	P(5)	*	*	*
Position of Stick (1 and 3 o'clock)				T(5)	*	*	*	*

Skills (*continued*)	Week 1 Day 1	Week 1 Day 2	Week 2 Day 1	Week 2 Day 2	Week 3 Day 1	Week 3 Day 2	Week 4 Day 1	Week 4 Day 2
Team Offense								
Cutting for the ball			T(5)	P(5)	*	*	*	*
Fast break				T(5)	P(5)	*	*	*
Spreading the attack				T(5)	P(5)	*	*	*
Critical scoring area				T(5)	P(5)	*	*	*
Free position on 8 meters				T(5)	P(5)	*	*	*
Free position on 12 meters				T(5)	P(5)	*	*	*
Team Defense								
Against fast break					T(5)	P(5)	*	*
Double team								T(5)
Crease defense			T(5)	P(5)	*	*	*	*
Defending a pick							T(5)	P(5)
Transition from clear							T(5)	P(5)
Communication	Emphasize with each new team concept.							
Goalkeeper†								
Positioning	T(10)	P(10)	*	*	*	*	*	*
Clearing	T(10)	P(10)	*	*	*	*	*	*
Saves	T(10)	P(10)	*	*	*	*	*	*
Rules	T(10)	P(10)	*	*	*	*	*	*

†An assistant coach should set up a warm-up and practice routine with goalies for each practice.

Appendix B

Sample Season Plan for Beginning Boys' Lacrosse Players

Goal: To help players learn and practice the individual skills and team tactics needed to play a lacrosse game successfully.

T(#) = Initial skill teaching time (minutes)   * = Skills practiced during drills and activities
P(#) = Review and practice time (minutes)

Skills	Week 1 Day 1	Week 1 Day 2	Week 2 Day 1	Week 2 Day 2	Week 3 Day 1	Week 3 Day 2	Week 4 Day 1	Week 4 Day 2
Warm-Up Exercises**	T(10)	P(10)	P(10)	P(10)	P(10)	P(10)	P(10)	P(10)
Cool-Down Exercises	T(5)	P(5)	P(5)	P(5)	P(5)	P(5)	P(5)	P(5)
Evaluation	(5)	(5)	(5)	(5)	(5)	(5)	(5)	(5)
Understanding the Game								
Player positions	T(5)	T(5)	*	*	*	*	*	*
Rules and penalties	T(5)	T(5)	T(5)	T(5)	*	*	*	*
Throwing								
Overhand technique	T(10)	P(5)	*	*	*	*	*	*
Right hand		T(5)	*	*	*	*	*	*
Left hand		T(5)	*	*	*	*	*	*
Catching								
Technique	T(1)	P(5)	*	*	*	*	*	*
Right hand, stick side		T(5)	P(5)	*	*	*	*	*
Right hand, off-stick side			T(5)	P(5)	*	*	*	*

**Athletes do additional warm-up before the official practice warm-up session begins.

	Week 1		Week 2		Week 3		Week 4	
	Day 1	Day 2	Day 1	Day 2	Day 1	Day 2	Day 1	Day 2
Skills (*continued*)								
Left hand, stick side		T(5)	P(5)	*	*	*	*	*
Left hand, off-stick side			T(5)	P(5)	*	*	*	*
Over the shoulder				T(5)	P(5)	*	*	*
Throwing and catching drills	P(10)	P(10)	P(10)	P(10)	P(10)	P(10)	P(10)	P(10)
Scooping								
Technique	T(10)	P(5)	*	*	*	*	*	*
Scooping and throwing			T(5)	P(5)	*	*	*	*
Scooping and give and go					T(5)	P(5)	*	*
Drills	P(5)	P(10)	P(10)	P(10)	P(10)	P(10)	P(10)	P(10)
Cradling								
Two-handed	T(5)	P(5)	P(5)	*	*	*	*	*
One-handed		T(5)	P(5)	P(5)	*	*	*	*
Shooting								
Outside			T(10)	P(5)	*	*	*	*
Inside			T(10)	P(5)	*	*	*	*
On the run					T(5)	P(5)	*	*
Off a cut					T(5)	P(5)	*	*
Drills			P(10)	P(10)	P(10)	P(10)	P(10)	P(10)
Individual Offense								
Face dodge		T(5)	P(5)	*	*	*	*	*
Roll dodge			T(5)	P(5)	*	*	*	*
Bull dodge				T(5)	P(5)	*	*	*
Inside roll					T(5)	P(5)	*	*

	Week 1		Week 2		Week 3		Week 4	
Skills *(continued)*	Day 1	Day 2	Day 1	Day 2	Day 1	Day 2	Day 1	Day 2
V cut	T(10)						T(5)	P(5)
Drills		P(5)	P(5)	P(5)	P(5)	P(5)	P(5)	P(5)
Unsettled Team Defense								
4-on-3 fast break					T(10)	P(5)	*	*
5-on-5 slow break							T(10)	T(5)
Drills					P(5)	P(5)	P(5)	P(5)
Settled Team Offense								
Dodging from the top					T(10)	T(10)	P(10)	P(10)
Midfield sweep					T(10)	T(10)	P(10)	P(10)
Dodging from behind					T(10)	T(10)	P(10)	P(10)
Extra man					T(10)	T(10)	P(10)	P(10)
Scrimmage					T(10)	T(10)	P(10)	P(10)
Riding								
Riding off a save							T(10)	P(10)
Settled riding							T(10)	P(10)
Individual Defense								
Ready position	T(10)	P(5)	*	*	*	*	*	*
Field position against a dodger (top, side, and behind)		T(10)	P(5)	*	*	*	*	*
Field position off the ball		T(10)	P(5)	*	T(10)	*	*	*
Poke and slap checks					T(10)	*	*	*
Playing on the crease						T(10)	P(5)	*
Drills	P(5)	P(5)	P(5)	P(5)	P(10)	P(10)	P(10)	P(10)

Skills (*continued*)	Week 1 Day 1	Week 1 Day 2	Week 2 Day 1	Week 2 Day 2	Week 3 Day 1	Week 3 Day 2	Week 4 Day 1	Week 4 Day 2
Settled Team Defense								
Field position off the ball					T(10)	T(10)	T(10)	T(10)
Sliding against a dodger (adjacent, cross-crease, and/or from the crease)								
Versus picks								
Versus cutters								
Scrimmage					P(10)	P(10)	P(10)	P(10)
Clearing								
Off a save							T(10)	P(10)
Settled clearing							T(10)	P(10)
Goalkeeper (Each save should be practiced on stick and off-stick sides.)								
Positioning	T(10)	P(10)	*	*	*	*	*	*
High save		T(10)	*	*	*	*	*	*
Hip save			T(10)	*	*	*	*	*
Low save				T(10)	*	*	*	*
Bounce save					T(10)	*	*	*
Drills	P(10)	P(10)	P(10)	P(10)	P(10)	P(10)	P(10)	
Communication	Emphasize with each new team concept.							

Appendix C

Girls' Lacrosse Officiating Signals

Time-out

Time-in

Blocking

Pushing

Rough check

Illegal check on body

Illegal ball off
body

Obstruction of
free space

Empty crosse
check

Goal circle foul

Free position
held whistle

Re-draw

Appendix D

Boys' Lacrosse Officiating Signals

Illegal body check

Slashing

Crosse checking

Tripping

Warding off

Holding

Stalling

Offsides

Crease violation

Play on

Appendix E

Organizations to Contact
for Coaching Children With Disabilities

American Athletic Association of the Deaf
3607 Washington Boulevard, Suite 4
Ogden, UT 84403-1737
(801) 393-8710
TTY: (801) 393-7916
Fax: (801) 393-2263

Disabled Sports USA
451 Hungerford Drive, Suite 100
Rockville, MD 20850
(301) 217-0960

Paralyzed Veterans of America
801 18th Street NW
Washington, DC 20006
(202) 872-1300
(800) 424-8200

Special Olympics International
1325 G Street NW, Suite 500
Washington, DC 20005
(202) 628-3630

U.S. Association of Blind Athletes
33 North Institute
Colorado Springs, CO 80903
(719) 630-0422

U.S. Cerebral Palsy Athletic Association
3810 West NW Highway, Suite 205
Dallas, TX 75220
(214) 351-1510

U.S. Les Autres Sports Association
1475 West Gray, Suite 166
Houston, TX 77019-4926
(713) 521-3737

ASEP Volunteer Level

The American Sport Education Program (ASEP) offers three Volunteer Level curriculums for adults who work with youth sport:

■ SportCoach ■ SportParent ■ SportDirector

SportCoach

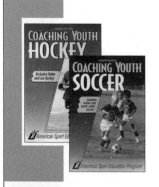

ASEP's SportCoach Program consists of two courses:

The **Rookie Coaches Course** provides inexperienced coaches with essential information for teaching the skills and strategies of a sport, including sample practice plans. Companion coaching guides are available for baseball, basketball, football, gymnastics, hockey, ski racing, softball, soccer, swimming, tennis, volleyball, and wrestling.

The **Coaching Young Athletes Course** is for second-year coaches and others who want more instruction in the principles of coaching than is offered in the Rookie Course.

SportParent

ASEP's SportParent Course is a 1- to 2-hour program that provides youth sport administrators and coaches with a practical and effective way to educate parents about their children's participation in sports.

The SportParent Course Package includes the *SportParent Facilitator Manual,* the *SportParent Video,* the *SportParent Survival Guide,* and the *SportParent* book.

SportDirector

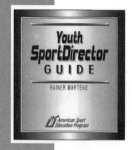

ASEP's SportDirector Program offers outstanding opportunities for youth sport directors to improve sport programs for the children in their community. The program includes a very practical *Youth SportDirector Guide* and a dynamic workshop.

American Sport Education Program

P.O. Box 5076
Champaign, IL 61825-5076
Fax: 217-351-1549

For more information on ASEP's Volunteer Level programs, call Toll-Free 1-800-747-5698.